Shanghai Tango

Jin Xing is one of China's foremost ballerinas; she is a mother of three and lives in Shanghai.

Shanghai Tango

A MEMOIR

JIN XING

With Catherine Texier

Atlantic Books
London

First published in France as *Rien N'arrive Par Hasard* in 2005 by Éditions Robert Laffont, 24 avenue Marceau, 75381 Paris Cedex 08.

First published in Great Britain in trade paperback in 2007 by Atlantic Books, an imprint of Grove Atlantic Ltd.

1 3 5 7 9 8 6 4 2

A CIP catalogue record for this book is available from the British Library.

ISBN 978 1 84354 632 0

Design by Helen Ewing
Printed in Finland

Atlantic Books
An imprint of Grove Atlantic Ltd
Ormond House
26–27 Boswell Street
London WC1N 3JZ

GOLDEN STAR

1

The jeep is parked in front of our house, in Beijing. I am sitting in the back, with filming equipment piled up next to me: a camera, mikes, cables and lighting paraphernalia. Li Xiaoming is in the front, holding another camera. He turns around to film me. Li Jian, the driver, is getting impatient: we're going to be late. Li Xiaoming asks him to wait a little longer because Mother has come out for a last goodbye and he wants to capture the moment on film. She is leaning against the door frame, tears running down her face. She makes no attempt to wipe them away. I have rarely seen her cry before and my heart aches at the sight now. She has devoted herself to me, her only son. In China, it's the son who continues the family line; the son who is showered with love; the son who matters most. And now she is about to lose her son and gain another daughter.

Li Jian taps his watch. 'We have to go.'

I signal him to start the engine. As the jeep pulls away, I turn around for a last look at my mother who is still standing stiffly at the door, her face anguished and broken, like her heart. I too start to cry. Li Xiaoming keeps the camera rolling. I tell myself that I am crying for my mother. But I know it's deeper than that. In just a few hours' time my whole life – my life at the army school, my life as a colonel, my life as a man; the only life I know – will change beyond anything I can imagine and there'll be no going back. I am pitching forward into an unknown darkness. Despite all the preparation I've done, analysing every last detail of the operation, weighing up the pros and cons, even buying a whole new, feminine wardrobe from the most glamorous boutiques Las Vegas has to offer, I still have no idea what my future will hold.

~~~

It is 1995 and we have just celebrated Chinese New Year. I turn twenty-eight in August. It's cold. Winter has dried up the earth outside the city and stripped the trees bare. The landscape, usually so cheerful in this area, feels gloomy. Does the car speed through it? Are there traffic jams on the way out of Beijing? I don't recall. I have been waiting for this moment for over twenty years.

At the Hospital of the Perfumed Hills, Dr Yang shows us her collection of silicone breasts. They come in all sizes: 200 grams, 250 grams, large and small. I pick them up one at a time. I prod the largest one with the tip of my finger as if I were shopping for fruit in a store. It is firm and plump. That's the one I want, but Dr Yang tries to dissuade me. She praises the elegance of the smallest one. No way! It is laughably flat, like the chest of a fifteen-year-old girl. I am twenty-seven; I need a real woman's bust. Li Xiaoming agrees. The bigger the better, no question. But Dr Yang won't be swayed. They would bother you when you dance, she says, exercising her medical authority. But I think she finds the large ones too provocative, too showy. A young Chinese woman must be discreet and that would not be easy if she were walking around with a pair of double-Ds. We reach a compromise and settle on a medium-sized cup.

It's a simple operation, the least painful of the three I will undergo. And in any case, I am in good hands with Dr Yang Peiying, who was the first surgeon to carry out breast augmentation in China and has a solid reputation.

At the hospital, I have a room to myself. I had to negotiate hard and wait an awfully long time to get it. They usually try to squeeze five or even seven patients into one room. Single rooms are reserved for dignitaries and high-ranking officers and the hospital administrator warned me that I would have to pay at least double the usual price to get one. I don't care. I would pay triple if necessary. It is like being in a hotel room: it is quiet and comes with a private bathroom, a personal nurse, a TV and a telephone. In short, it is deluxe, and above all else I want to be comfortable. Plastic surgery patients are rare over the Chinese New Year period and the hospital is only too happy to make a little money on the side rather than leave a room empty. The film crew have rented the room next door to stash their equipment (there are three cameras and six crew) and Li Xiaoming will be able to sleep there too.

Before I'm allowed anywhere near the scalpel, I must take a psychology test at Beijing Medical University's Third Hospital. Compared to the rigorous requirements of western hospitals – two years of psychotherapy, followed by a 'real life' test, during which you must live dressed as a woman – this sounds easy enough. But I still have to convince the doctors that I am a good candidate for sex reassignment surgery. I am eager to tackle the thousand-odd dry, yes-or-no type questions. They are cleverly designed to catch you out, subtly rephrasing and reiterating each point, but I'm ready for them. If only 60 per cent of your answers come up as 'feminine', you will not qualify for the operation. If you hit 75 per cent, you are encouraged to undergo 're-masculinization' therapy – something I must avoid at all costs. Above 80 per cent and surgery is recommended. I shoot for 80 per cent. The result exceeds my expectations: 94 per cent. The medical authorities give me the green light.

Theatre. The lights are blinding. Men in white overalls scurry about. 'Why so many doctors?' I think to myself as I survey the room. Then I realize that it's the film crew, dressed in surgeons' scrubs. Dr Yang has given them permission to film the operation, and they're setting up the lighting equipment. Watching them bustle about, it is as if they're getting a stage ready for a show. The thought is strangely comforting and suddenly I feel at ease.

'*Shang tai*,' Dr Yang says. 'Climb up.'

I have to laugh. In Chinese, the expressions 'to climb onto the operating table' and 'to go onstage' are the same.

'OK,' I say to myself. 'If I'm to be on stage, I shall simply treat this as my next performance.'

Dr Yang leans towards me.

'Ready?'

'Ready!'

She nods. I lie down. The cameras are trained on me. I am no longer afraid.

'Cameras! Action!'

The next day, back in my private room, I look at my profile in the mirror. A feminine image greets me. I cup my hands around my new breasts, astonished. I can't believe that I have made the first step! I know there is still a long way to go; after the next operation the pain will be intense, and after the third and last one it will be almost unbearable. But I don't think about that just yet. I trace my nipples with a finger, admiring their delicate curves, filled with wonder. My childhood dream is finally becoming reality.

I am six years old. I have just come home after watching a perform-ance of *The White-Haired Girl*, one of communist China's first major ballets. It tells the story of a young girl who flees a bullying landowner and ends up hiding in a cave, where her hair turns white. She is eventually rescued by the People's Liberation Army, of course. I am intoxicated with joy, thrilled by the principal dancer's graceful movements and the easy flow of her jetés. Her sparkling costume is entrancing, and I am mesmerized by the way her long tresses glide and swing every time she leaps and by the mysterious glow of her pale make-up. It's a world away from the shows I get to perform in kindergarten, shows like *The Legend of the Red Lantern*, an opera in which all I do is stand rigid onstage and sing of the glory of the revolutionary hero Li Yuhe.

Back home, I climb up onto my *kang*, my brick sleeping platform, and pull away the blankets. I peel off a pillowcase and wrap it around my forehead like a headdress, twisting it at the nape of my neck to fashion a kind of braid. Then I twirl round and round, pretending I am the white-haired heroine. That night, I dream of a terrible storm. A torrential downpour courses through the streets; flashes of lightning sear the night sky with silver zigzags so bright it seems like daytime; thunder shakes the walls. I dream that a thunderbolt hits me and – whoosh! – I become a girl with long, long hair. I never want to wake up… and I have been waiting, ever since, for that bolt from the blue to make my wish come true.

Back in the real world I am a young boy again, living with my mother and my elder sister. We lodge with an old lady in a small Manchurian village about a hundred kilometres from Shenyang, the capital of Liaoning province. My parents are both Korean émigrés. My mother and her sister fled Korea during the war, which had killed both their parents and their only brother. They sought refuge in northern China. It was there that she met my father, a handsome, older officer in the People's Liberation Army of China, who dazzled the little orphan girl. My sister Jin Xianglan was born in 1964 and I followed in 1967.

Now, six years on, we are in the middle of the Cultural Revolution and my father works for the Regional War Office in Shenyang. The Red Guard denied my mother permission to live with him, so we see him only rarely. I remember him as a shadowy figure during my early childhood, someone who appeared from time to time, a distant presence, seemingly indifferent to his wife and children. Later, when we eventually moved to Shenyang to be with him, I recall dismal family outings, with him walking far out in front of us, alone, while we traipsed along behind at a respectful distance. He is a 'red': in the army his nickname is Jin the Marxist–Leninist. My mother, however, is regularly accused of being a spy – in part because she is Korean and works as a Japanese translator, but also because when she first came to China she was given shelter by a known traitor. As a result, she must undergo interminable interrogations by the Red Guard each and every night. In retrospect, I can see why my father tried to keep his distance.

But at the time I knew nothing about that. All I knew was that my universe was full of women who adored and cherished me. The village house we lived in with the old lady was simple, but Mother always kept it impeccably clean even though she returned home exhausted from her self-criticism sessions. Every morning, the old lady would take me to the edge of the village to watch the peasants toiling, bent double, in the rice paddies. She had beautiful eyes – cat's eyes, keen and full of love. I relished the freedom of the countryside. I remember rides in the horse-drawn cart and the inky blackness of the night sky – I could never work out whether it held demons or gods, and the thought fascinated me even though we did not practise any religion. I loved to attend country funerals and watch the paper offerings being set aflame; the mournful songs they sang sent me into raptures and I always disobeyed the old lady's entreaties to return home. She would tell me stories of will-o'-the-wisps that would kidnap disobedient children, but I would not budge. The flames would burst out, flicker and fly off into the night like spirits or sprites. They were alive to me, like fairytales come true. I would linger until the last of the blazes died down and the night came to rest upon us, crackling and velvety.

One of my mother's colleagues, whom I called Auntie Zhang, often came to visit us. She had beautiful long braids that coiled down the length of her back and rested, regally, on the stiff little collar of her jacket, like quivering grass snakes. While Mother made tea, I would play with her hair, undoing and re-plaiting it.

'Xing, you're going to mess up Auntie Zhang's hair,' Mother would say, exasperated.

'Oh, let him be, he's enjoying it so.'

My sister Xianglan made fun of me, though. At nine, she knew that boys were not supposed to do that. I did not care.

My mother's friends would whisper, 'Look at Jin Xing, he looks like a little girl, not a little boy!'

'Oh, he'll get over it,' Mother would say, 'he's still a baby.'

There were other ways in which I did not behave like the other boys when I was a kid. The boxes of firecrackers my father's friends gave me remained unopened; I was too scared to play with them, and much preferred playing girls' games like skipping, dressing up and hopscotch. I used to wear my sister's hand-me-downs. The printed quilt jackets, so bright and lovely on Xianglan, were stained dark blue for me, and the colourful trousers became almost funereal. They were gruesome. 'I'd rather die,' I'd wail when it came to getting dressed, but Mother could not be swayed. She could be so gentle, but when I challenged her she would not give in. She simply handed me a pair of the newly dyed trousers and told me to get dressed without making a fuss. 'You are a boy,' she told me, 'and I will not dress you up as a girl.' We were always as stubborn as each other, and still are today.

Until the age of three, I went to the women's baths with my mother, as is the custom in China. But when I turned five, whenever my father came to visit, and later when we moved in with him in Shenyang, he took me to the men's baths. How uncomfortable I felt among the hairy creatures there! Sometimes, though, a beautiful young man would walk in, and I remember how I would become aroused at the sight. These were my first sexual experiences, confused and wonderful amidst the steam of the baths. As young as I was, though, I knew it was something I must keep secret.

One day, after we had moved to Shenyang, a young friend of my mother who worked in a weaving factory invited us to visit her family in the country. Her elder brother was there and his beauty took my breath away. He was tall and well built, with soft hair hanging down over his smoky eyes – a dark, sensual face, with the sexiest sideburns I had ever seen. I could not take my eyes off him... The boys I saw at the baths were nothing in comparison. But there was something else about this boy – he returned my glances. His looks were not merely amused or tender; they were seductive, out of the corner of his eyes. We stayed overnight and I had to share the brother's bed. As I listened to him fall asleep, his breathing becoming slow and deep in the dark, I realized I was listening to the powerful, even breaths of a man. I was happier than I had ever been.

⟶

We moved to Shenyang to be with my father when my mother finally received authorization to live with him. It was not difficult for her to find work; she was quickly hired as an archivist at the Light

Industry Research Centre. At that time my father was working in the cartography department of Military Intelligence. Family life would not last long though; Father would soon be transferred to Dalian, leaving us alone yet again.

My passions were still dancing and singing. At the Shenyang army kindergarten my reputation grew so fast that a TV crew came to film a documentary about me, the little rising star. Maybe my name sealed my fate: Jin Xing means Golden Star in Chinese. When I left the kindergarten to enrol in year one at the Korean school, I was quickly selected for the dance troupe, which comprised eighteen girls and just two boys. This did not go unnoticed by my classmates.

'Hey you, you're a girl!' they would tease as I walked by fully made-up for a performance.

'Hey, your brother's a girl,' they taunted Xianglan.

I would make my sister give me piggy-back rides to and from school so that I didn't have to walk through the slushy snow for an hour and a half. One day, on the way home, with my arms clutched around her neck and my legs wrapped around her waist, and straining under the further weight of her book bag, Xianglan delivered her killer blow.

'The boys in my class say that you're a girl.'

I dug my knees into her ribs like a jockey spurring on his mount. 'So?'

She glanced at me over her shoulder. Her face was red and dripping with sweat and her hair hung down in bedraggled wet locks from under her cap, which was covered in a thin layer of snow. With a heave she tried to throw me off, but I clung on. She walked on.

'You should quit dancing.'

'Why?'

'Don't you think you're a little old for that? I mean, for a boy?'

Another heave, but I held tight.

'No way. Anyway, it's none of your business.'

'It is my business since you're my brother. I don't like it that they say my brother is a girl.'

'So what? I do like it.'

'You don't know what you're talking about. Get off, you're too heavy.'

'No. Keep going. We're almost there anyway.'

My mother did not try to discourage me from dancing when I was young. Maybe she thought that I would grow out of it, along with my other girlish ways. I was just a kid, after all, and I should have fun. One thing she would never let me get away with, though, was being lazy and neglecting my schoolwork – for which she would punish me harshly. God knows, she had plenty of opportunity. I never did my homework. I could never see the point of wearing myself out over my notebooks when playing was so much more engrossing. As soon as Mother's back was turned, I would make a bolt for it, often running over to the neighbours who had just bought a little black-and-white TV. I loved to watch the announcements gliding across the screen in a continuous loop: they utterly fascinated me. Soon enough, Mother would track me down and drag me back home by my ear, administering a few clouts with her wooden spoon as soon as the door was closed. She was angry for my disobedience, and ashamed because we could not afford a TV of our own. With the red welts on my backside still smarting from the beating, I would sneak back to the neighbours' place. I was always a rebel, always defying authority: strong-willed, stubborn and, above all, restless.

2

I am at school, in the middle of a gym class – five hundred kids doing their stretches in the playground. We are busy sweating and puffing when five People's Liberation Army officers in full uniform – three men and two women – appear alongside the gym teacher. The teacher explains that they have come to select the most talented students for the local PLA dance troupe.

In a flash I know the truth: they are here for *me*! They must have seen the TV documentary. My heart almost explodes in my chest. Somehow I force myself to concentrate and get on with my stretches as if nothing were happening. Sure enough, a few minutes later, my name hisses through the loudspeaker. 'Jin Xing! Jin Xing is called to the director's office!' All eyes are fixed on me as I cross the playground proud as a peacock with my chest puffed out, walking bolt upright like the letter 'I' – an apt comparison: this is my moment. Everybody knows that if you are selected, you go to the army school. I am even more aware than the others of what this means, my father being an army officer. It is a true honour. It is brilliant!

The following day, the same officers show up at our home. I watch them arrive from my bedroom window. Again I feel my heartbeat quicken. They introduce themselves to my parents, polite as anything, and in return they are invited inside to talk. One of the officers explains that they have been most impressed by my talent and they would like to invite me to join the army school's dance troupe. I can hardly bear to listen. The atmosphere is tense. My father lights a cigarette, and remains quiet for a moment while he takes a deep, pensive drag, exhales, and then finally says, 'OK. Fine. The army school offers a good education.'

It takes all of my willpower to keep my composure – I want to yelp and whoop and jump up and down right there in the middle of the room!

But no sooner have the words left my father's mouth than my mother, who has always supported my artistic activities – my mother, whom I believed was my ally – shuffles and straightens up in her chair, draws her lips tight and, without even looking at my father, retorts, 'Absolutely not. My son will go to university. He will be neither a singer nor a dancer. It is no career for a boy.'

I can't believe my ears. I refuse to believe it. Surely Father has said OK? Surely that seals it? But in the silence that follows, I see that Mother's word is final. The glorious future I have imagined for myself as a dancer and member of the People's Liberation Army goes up in smoke, just like the paper offerings I used to watch fizzle and die at the country funerals all those years ago.

Singing and dancing are my whole life; her cruel words have killed something inside me. I can hold my tongue no longer. 'But Mother, I want to go! Please let me go. *Please*,' I plead.

Mother makes her stubborn face. 'Shut up. You don't know what you're talking about.'

The officers, caught in the middle of our battle, don't know how to react. Awkwardly they get up, make their excuses and say good-bye. I have never known such despair. I cry. I scream. I sob hard, like a baby, unashamed. I cannot be consoled. With hatred in my heart I resolve, there and then, not to let them win.

I try every trick in the book, even refusing to go to school. But Mother does not give in. Once again we have locked horns: stalemate. I promise myself that she will not have the last word this time. I have a genius idea. I lie down on my *kang*, pull the blankets up to my chin and refuse to move. I won't eat a thing until they agree to let me go. I'm so upset that I don't feel hungry, anyway.

That evening, as I am falling asleep, I hear them talking to each other in low voices.

'He has to eat. Take him a bowl of rice at least,' says Father.

Xianglan agrees. 'Give Little Brother something to eat. He's going to get sick.'

But Mother will hear none of it. 'If he won't eat, he won't eat. Too bad. It's his problem.'

Succulent aromas drift all the way upstairs to me. I can't help it – I am suddenly gripped by the most unbelievable hunger pangs. My stomach growls, my mouth salivates; but I clench my teeth tight. I'd rather die. I *must* win.

Father's the first to give in. On the evening of the second day he comes and sits on my bed, a piece of paper in his hand. 'Listen, Jin Xing, this is what we've decided. You can go to the army school if it's really what you want. It's your life, after all. But I warn you: army life is very, very hard. You are going to have a rough time. We will let you choose, but your decision is also your responsibility.' He hands me the piece of paper and a pencil. 'You will write a letter in which you will specify that army school was your decision and you promise you won't regret it. Do you understand?'

It is late, almost eleven o'clock, but I will not go to sleep until this letter is written, even if it takes me all night. I scribble, erase, start again, cross out… It must be perfect.

Dear Parents,
I swear it was me who chose to join the army school's dance troupe.
I take complete responsibility for that decision. I will never regret it.
I pledge to excel as an army dancer and to serve my country and the
Communist Party.
  Your son,
    JIN XING

The next morning I show the letter to my father. He glances at it but doesn't look happy. His mouth tightens.

'Hmmm…'

What did I do wrong? I have written quite a few self-criticisms before and I used the same style here. Was that a mistake? He hands me back the paper.

'Your handwriting is atrocious. Do it again.'

I apply myself to rewriting the letter, two copies this time, one for my family, the other for the director of the dance troupe, with whom my parents must meet before I can be accepted.

The director is a career officer. He does not know anything about dance, or even care that much about art. His only concern is that the dance troupe epitomize the glory and greatness of the People's Liberation Army. They perform propaganda dances and they must conform to a very specific physical ideal – the men must be tall and strong. Which is why, when he meets my parents, he suddenly becomes jittery. They are both short. And as for me, let's not even go there: I am not exactly what you would call strapping. The officer stumbles over his words and tries not to cause offence.

'You two are, well, you're not very tall, do you see what I mean? And your son, well, your son is still young for sure, but looking at you both I would think the chances are that he won't grow much taller than you. One never knows, true, but still… '

'You see,' my mother says, as we walk back home, 'we did what you wanted and let you go. But they don't want you. So forget about it.'

She can barely disguise her relief. There is even a spring in her step.

I, on the other hand, feel wretched. Most humiliating of all, after having bragged all about my success, I now have to go back to school with my tail between my legs. As I slip on my jacket and strap my book bag over my shoulder, I concoct an explanation that will save face in front of my classmates. On my way to school I run it over and over in my head: 'The army is not bad, sure, but all things considered, it's not as good as university. I'll have a better future there.'

But fate is not so easily flouted. A week later, we are yet again called to a meeting at the army school. I can't imagine why they would need to put me through the agony all over again, but still I must attend. The news couldn't be better. One of the thirty kids who was selected for the new troupe has been forced to withdraw because his parents are being transferred to Beijing. This leaves a last-minute vacancy, and with the new term about to begin the dance teachers have finally managed to convince the director that my extraordinary talent and promise as a dancer justifies bending the rules regarding physical requirements. I'm in!

My mother and I walk home in silence. Her footsteps sound heavier this time. Our building is close to the school, barely ten minutes' walk away. I feel that, at last, she has resigned herself to my future, my new direction. Now nothing is going to stop me from embracing military life. That evening I lie down on my *kang*, close my eyes and picture myself onstage, surrounded by lights, thunderous applause and flowers: a star dancer at last.

The following day, the director and the troupe's dance teachers visit us at home to discuss the conditions of my enrolment.

'Go and play, Jin Xing. Leave us alone.'

I am so excited that I run down the stairs at top speed and climb onto one of the bicycles balancing on the stand in front of our building. I don't know how to ride a bike yet, but that doesn't stop me from performing some perilous acrobatics on the stationary vehicle, acting like I'm mounting a stubborn mule. But I am too wild and unruly and, as if in slow motion, the bike tips sideways, I lose my balance and crash down hard onto my elbow, which gets caught under the bicycle frame and breaks. Imagine my parents' faces when they rush down, just having signed the enrolment forms. Not to mention the faces of the director and the dance teachers! I can see they are wondering if they've made a terrible mistake; their new recruit, barely hired, is already crippled.

There were thirteen of us boys, aged between nine and seventeen, and I was the youngest and smallest of the lot. If that wasn't enough to mark me out from the crowd, my arm was in a sling. At night, we all slept like spoons alongside each other, seven boys in one bed and six in another, packed in like sardines in a tin.

On the very first night we had barely dropped off when an alarm sounded and woke us all up.

'Enemy on the way!' came the cry.

'What enemy?' I said. 'What kind of a stupid joke is this?' And then I went right back to sleep. Talk about starting out on the wrong foot! I had a lot to learn.

The official wake-up call was at 5.30 a.m. Our blankets had to be tucked in with corners as sharp as blocks of tofu and our caps lined up perfectly on top, with our toothpaste tubes and toothbrushes arranged in a neat row beside them. Then there was jogging, followed by an hour of indoor gymnastics. And then stretches – which was when the torture commenced.

The gym was in a large auditorium, its ceiling supported by towering pillars. We were arranged into pairs and told to stand against a pillar, one on either side. The instruction came to stretch a leg up against the column until we were all doing the vertical splits. Then, a series of pulleys were lowered from the ceiling next to each student and, to my horror, the teacher proceeded to attach them to our outstretched legs before giving the signal for the pulley to yank back upwards – pulling our legs with them! Once at maximum stretch, our legs were bound to our pillar with rope and we were told to stand like that for fifteen minutes before resuming the torture again on the opposite leg. For two or three minutes you could hold it; it hurt, but it was bearable. After that, the ligaments started to rip and it was pure hell. Oh, I will never forget those screams as long as I live – like pigs being butchered! The girls were more stoical, their groans of agony more controlled, more discreet; but the boys did not hold back. Every morning, from 6.30 a.m. to 7.30 a.m., it sounded like a slaughterhouse in there.

We would change into our uniforms for breakfast, eat in silence, then change back into gym gear. At 8 a.m. it was time for Russian ballet and Beijing Opera acrobatics (a traditional form of dance), and after that came lunch (back in uniform), followed by a nap. In the afternoon we had folk dancing class, Beijing Opera class and, finally, drama class. On three afternoons we did schoolwork.

My problem was not with the training, but with the discipline. To eat without saying a word was beyond me – and indeed it would be still; I chatter like a magpie. We were expected to empty our plates as fast as possible, so in order not to waste any time I would talk with my mouth full. Yak, yak, yak, I would gabble on, spluttering bits of food onto my neighbour's plate as I did. I was always the noisy one.

During nap time that first day, I got up and crept out of the dorm to play. I was nine: how could I be expected to behave like a seventeen-year-old? I just could not help testing the boundaries, even though I knew how it would inevitably end – with the words, 'Jin Xing! Your self-criticism – now!'

I found a pencil and a piece of paper and began to write. It was during my time in the army that I become an expert at self-criticism. It all started when I surreptitiously read *Chronicle of Strange Marriages*, a love story about two couples written during the Tang Dynasty, a book that didn't exactly feature on the list authorized by Chairman Mao – and it went on from there! So I knew the self-criticism formulas by heart. I learnt that if I used a whole bunch of them, it looked more convincing: 'I lack self-discipline; I don't have enough respect for the education provided by the government; I pledge to train harder and to work more, even more than my classmates.' I piled it on, even promising: 'I pledge to be the best of all the students. I beg you, give me another chance to prove myself, I will not disappoint you, I promise.' I handed the paper to my supervisor. There we go! Matter closed.

The army school was a boarding school and although my family lived nearby, I was not allowed to go home. Rules are rules, and rules were everything in the army. It would demoralize the other students if I was granted special favours. In three years, I was allowed back home only once. Occasionally, on summer evenings, my parents and my sister would stroll over to watch me in the school playground as I jumped around like a monkey in a zoo. Sometimes I would catch sight of them and bolt over to the school gates. Even though I promised that I would take responsibility for myself, I grab on to the bars of the gate like a miserable little prisoner.

Xianglan would cry and beg my parents, 'Mum, Dad, Little Brother is much too young to be locked in like that. You have no heart.'

But my father would shake his head. It was my choice, after all. And he had the letter to prove it.

My mother never spoke. But her silence told me all I needed to know: she still disapproved.

I loved Russian ballet and excelled at folk dancing. But that was the girls' speciality and whereas most of their time was devoted to it, we boys concentrated on floor exercises which I found deadly dull. As soon as the teacher left the room, I would scamper off to hang out with the girls, pirouetting on the other side of the curtain which divided our classes in two. I felt so much more comfortable with them. They treated me as their mascot, their little brother, and when I was with them I felt like I was at the very heart of things. I used to watch them so intently that I came to know their dance routines by heart and, rascal that I was, I would even correct them – which of course annoyed them no end. But they didn't hold grudges for long – because I was valuable to them in other, more important ways: I knew all the boys' gossip.

At night, from my spot at the end of the bed, I could listen to them whispering to each other.

'Did you see M—? She's getting big boobs!'

'Too big, she's becoming podgy.'

'And what about Y—? Check out that arse…'

'Yeah, she's a babe. I'd do her.'

And so on.

The next day I would trot right off and repeat everything I'd overheard to the girls. I was their spy.

We have to learn to become real soldiers, like the other army recruits, and so twice a year during our first years at the school, we boys go on two-month-long manoeuvres with our base unit. They are my worst nightmare: I am nine, I am small, I am skinny, and I feel like a little girl hiding inside a boy's body. How do I play this macho role convincingly? Don't count on me to defend the People's Republic! The school director who thought I was too puny was right: I am not cut from a soldier's cloth.

First there's the uniform: the waistband of the trousers comes up to my neck and the jacket sleeves hang below my fingertips. I look like a soldier on a comedy show, hems pooling around my ankles and my khaki red-star cap flopping over my eyes. Mother has to take the clothes away and make alterations before I can so much as walk in them without tripping up or heading straight into a wall.

Then there is the gun, which is taller than I am by seven or eight centimetres and too long to strap across my chest. I have to drag it along behind me and it bumps around on the pebbles as we march like it's alive. We start each day with a half-hour shooting exercise: standing, lying down, squatting. I ask the captain if I can stay lying down, as I am unable to lift my weapon, even with both hands. 'OK,' he says, once he's convinced himself that I'm telling the truth. Half an hour later, he's shaking me by my shoulders like a dusty cloth. I must have fallen asleep alongside my gun. I have missed the whole shooting practice.

We end the session with the hand grenades. Once the pin is out, we have exactly ten seconds to run for cover before it explodes. I don't have a lot of strength in my shoulders so I can't toss it very far, and I am terrified of dropping it too close to my feet and blowing myself up. I beg the captain to let me skip my turn. But no, it's an order. I move forward, legs wobbly, shaking from head to toe, clutching my grenade. I throw it as far as I can and run back on the double. By the count of eight I am already flat on the ground, nose in the dust. One minute later, still no explosion. I lift my head.

'Jin Xing, when you go down don't move a muscle. Did you even pull the pin?' the captain roars.

I look at him blankly. I haven't the faintest idea.

'Go back and get it!'

I drag myself back, crying my eyes out. Exasperated, the captain finally grabs the grenade out of my hand. Of course, the pin is still intact.

'Get the hell out of here and write your self-criticism!'

But the self-criticism doesn't satisfy him. He glances at the paper, crumples it up and shoves me back into line. I've got to go one more time. I shake my head stubbornly, wiping my tears with the back of my hand. We are all standing in line and the one who's due to go next is getting antsy. He leans towards me and whispers, 'Stop crying. You're going to make us lose face!'

I move forward again. I'm shaking so hard that the group leader holds my hand and helps me pull the pin out of my grenade. I run for cover just a few steps back and flatten myself to the floor yet again. The group leader shelters me as the grenade explodes, a few metres away from us, with a deafening boom. I am unharmed but ashamed; my cheeks burn red.

I take my revenge by winning the speed competition: dismantling and reassembling my rifle in less than a minute in the dark.

⌒つ

We are on manoeuvres near Dandong, in the mountains of northern Manchuria. The town has been devastated by huge floods and our regiment has been dispatched to help with relief work. It's my fourth year at the army school; I am thirteen. We haven't even reached Dandong yet because a landslide has blocked a tunnel and our train can't get through. We are stranded in the middle of a forest, with no visible sign of life for miles around – not even a peasant! Every day our team gets to work as early as 3 a.m., digging through the mud to clear the tunnel. In the evening we barbecue our meat supplies and sleep in the train's berths.

As I am the youngest, the colonel who heads our troupe (and who has taken a shine to me) allows me to stay and look after the wagons instead of digging and building dams with the others. It's 6 a.m. I get up, button my uniform, strap my machine gun and two revolvers across my chest – I am hardly any more sturdily built than I was when I enrolled, but I have certainly learnt how to handle the equipment more skilfully. Fully togged up, I go and inspect each wagon. It is summertime: the weather is warm, the mountain air smells pure and the birds chirp their silvery, high-pitched calls.

When I reach the third carriage, I notice a hand dangling down from one of the upper berths. Someone must have overslept. I climb the ladder to take a closer look and find our company secretary: I know him well. He is older than we are, nineteen or twenty, and as a mere office worker he has not been sent out with the dig either. I watch him sleep for a moment. I don't know why, but his beauty moves me. Very gently I pick up the blanket that covers him. He is naked underneath the sheets. I have never seen a man's erect penis before. He opens his eyes and looks at me without saying anything. I don't know what to do. His gaze seems out of focus, as if he were still half-asleep. He grabs me abruptly, pulls me to him, takes my hand and slips it along his penis. I let him do it. I feel uncomfortable and yet I find that I myself have become aroused. Suddenly my hand is covered with a sticky fluid. I look at him but his eyes are closed again, as if he's gone back to sleep. I climb down the ladder. Did I do something wrong? I glance back at him over my shoulder as I reach the cabin door. He is still pretending to be asleep. I run out of the car. So that's what a man feels like. I have had erections before, of course, but to think that a man would want to be caressed by another man… That, I had never imagined.

We return from manoeuvres worn out and with our skin burnt black as coal by the sun. Back in the barracks, I can't stop thinking about the secretary. He smiles at me when he sees me and I am desperate to be his friend… but I also avoid him, because I feel I have done something wrong. In China, boys are not supposed to behave like that. Yet he has fully awoken my sexuality. Sometimes when I dance with older partners from the troupe, I feel their penis swell against me, but I am sure those are boys who like girls. I used to think that the way they held me tight in their arms was an expression of their affection towards me as a child. Now I see it's about something else. It's intoxicating to arouse the desire of those men. But why me? What is it about me that attracts them? I must project a kind of femininity which stirs them. Slowly I am coming to understand my self, my body, my nature – but I still can't put it into words. Nor would I speak them even if I could.

Butterflies Love Flowers is a major revolutionary ballet inspired by a poem by Mao Zedong, and we were to tour China with it that year. In one of the key scenes, Mao hands out weapons to the peasants: the male dancers hold a sickle and an axe, while the girls appear holding sprays of flowers for the Mountain Flower Dance. I was to dance cross the stage distributing weapons to the boys and flowers to the girls. After months of rehearsals, for me our opening performance is a disaster – waiting in the wings, confused amid the mess of flowers, sickles, axes and other weapons all piled up waiting for me,

I hastily grab two grenades, make my way onstage, and thrust them mistakenly into one of the girls' hands. The poor thing has to do her whole performance waving grenades instead of geraniums. Afterwards, she is inconsolable with the humiliation: my only excuse is that I am 'the little one', and it is beginning to lose currency,

Despite my blunder, the ballet is a great success that night, and at every performance we give across China. So much so, in fact, that Changchun Studios, the so-called Hollywood of Manchuria, offer to film it for us. I love being at the studios and spend as much of my spare time as I can aimlessly wandering around the lots. One afternoon after the daily shoot is over, I happen to discover an empty projection room. I sneak inside and settle down in front of the screen. They are showing a Soviet film of a classical ballet that I am sure we have studied, though I can't recall the name. After a few minutes I recognize the music of *Swan Lake*. The ballet is so gorgeous and the prima ballerina moves with such grace that I stay until the very end. As I'm about to leave, a new ballet appears on the screen; I shuffle down lower in my seat, hoping that nobody will notice me and, indeed, I am left undisturbed. Perhaps the projectionist is showing these films for his own pleasure. I go back the next day and this time it's a Chinese film of a play entitled *Miss Liu the Ingenious*. The star's beauty and the elegant simplicity of her acting fascinate me and again I stay until the end. When the credits roll I read her name: Xin Fengxia. From then on I go to the projection room every afternoon and watch all the films: comedies, dramas, filmed ballets. I am still dreaming of becoming a star one day, of being that prima ballerina filmed in close-up, performing elegant jetés, weaving a kind of magic over the audience watching from the stalls.

When filming is over, the studios arrange a concert in our honour. It is the violin concerto *Liang Shanpo and Zhu Yingtai*, about two star-crossed lovers. It's the first time I've been to a concert and I find it so moving that I begin to imagine how I would stage it as a ballet.

After our visit to Changchun, the studios continue to send us films of other ballets and I watch them avidly. The Soviet dancers are dazzling. I long to perform in the USSR and show them what I, too, am capable of. Every time I watch these films, I am transported to a fantasy world, and returning to the drab reality of the army school corridors is difficult. I have no idea how to make my dreams come true, and yet my dreams are as real to me as anything I know. I cheer myself up with pep talks, administering reprimands and encouragement in equal measure. I, Jin Xing, will also one day be one of the greats: but I must prepare myself well. I have a feeling that the moment will present itself to me just once and, when it comes, I must seize it with both hands. I sense that there are turning points in life that one cannot afford to miss.

By the age of thirteen I had attained my middle-school diploma. My problem remained my size. At 1.4 metres tall, I was still much too short to perform any of the lead roles, and on top of that I was terribly scrawny and my head appeared huge perched on top of my sparrow-like frame – in fact my nickname was 'Big Head'! I would train with the troupe during the mornings, but when afternoon rehearsals came my only role was to help with the costumes, make-up and hair. I was a long way indeed from fulfilling my dreams of becoming a prima but, nevertheless, I did not go unnoticed in my supporting role. Make-up artists marvelled at my deftness. Gradually I became involved in all the hidden backstage details of a performance, from arranging the lighting to choosing the colour of the earrings.

The troupe's director, the great classical Chinese choreographer

Mr Men Wenyan, took me under his wing. During morning rehearsals he put me in charge of the music. It was my job to start the cassettes playing, keep them in good order, and to suggest appropriate music for each piece. On top of that, I served as his muse. He would have me 'road-test' all of his new dances, both the girls' and the boys' roles, so that he could perfect them. I learnt my first choreographic techniques from him, and tried out my first female roles under his tutelage.

It was indeed an honour to be singled out by Mr Men, yet I did not trust him. Although married with three children, it was well known that he was gay. People said that the marriage was simply a front, to stop idle tongues from wagging. Gossip was one thing, but I knew he was homosexual... Let's say some of the things he did went beyond what's appropriate between a teacher and a student. He was a middle-aged man, well into his forties, older than my father even, so I tried to keep a respectful attitude. Every time he came too close to me, every time he tried to trap me against a door or on a couch, I would slip away, without making a big deal out of it. I could never dream of doing anything which would embarrass him or make him lose face: he was a very well-known teacher, after all. And would anyone have listened to me, even if I had? On occasion he would invite me to his place during the school naptime – always while his wife was out at work and his children at school – on some pretext like wanting me to listen to some music he was thinking of using for a new piece of choreography. But I was smart – I was on to him and I found excuses: I was tired, I had a rehearsal in the afternoon, sometimes I asked a classmate to come with me.

But it was not so easy to escape Mr Men's attentions. When we were on tour he arranged things so that we slept in the same room. Those in the know would snigger and make fun of me.

'Hey, Jin Xing, the boss has got his eye on you!'

'Come off it, you idiot!'

I pretended not to care, but in the evenings I would hang out in my classmates' bedrooms and turn in as late as possible, when Mr Men was fast asleep. I opened the door without a sound, padded across the room in my socks and lay down on top of my blanket with all my clothes still on. I was terrified of what would happen when I was asleep. I was attracted to men, sure, but the thought of having a sexual relationship with an old man of my father's generation was appalling.

When he realized that he was getting nowhere, he resorted to a kind of psychological blackmail. He threatened to drop me as his assistant, telling me he would get someone prettier, more docile, more talented than me. He stopped talking to me altogether, ignoring me until I paid more attention. By setting his sights on another favourite, he thought he could make me jealous and worry about losing my privileged position as teacher's pet. He misjudged me. I simply breathed a sigh of relief. We continued our precarious duet for years. He was a great ballet master, Mr Men, and in many ways I really loved him. As a choreographer and teacher, he was a remarkable man, but he made the mistake of confusing admiration with desire. I spent years tiptoeing around him – I had so much to learn from him, and he had such a lot of power.

In spite of Mr Men's support, and I think he genuinely believed in my talent, the directors of the troupe were pushing me to join the scenic arts team. They just did not see me as a principal dancer: my physique was not manly enough. It took a phone call from Song Zhaokun, one of my former teachers, to save me from this dead-end. She had been transferred to the People's Liberation Army Arts Institute in Beijing and invited me to continue my studies with her. I was flabbergasted. In my young, provincial mind Beijing shone like a shooting star, way beyond the grasp of a mere mortal like myself – and besides, I belonged to the Shenyang work unit and, legally, I was not allowed to switch. But Song Zhaokun insisted and somehow – I still don't know how – she convinced the local administrator and the troupe director to let me go.

3

Beijing, 9.30 p.m. I push firmly against the dorm door and enter the room. The lights are all off, everybody's in bed, still asleep like hens! I stand in the middle of the room, cup my hands around my mouth, forming a kind of loudspeaker and announce:

'Hey, kids! We're in Beijing and you're asleep? The streets are all lit up! Beijing is a great city! Nothing like Shenyang! Come on, get up!'

No answer. I turn around and leave. The school playground is deserted, all the lights are off. It's depressing. I go back inside, walk into the next dorm and start my little number again.

'Hey, kids! I've got something to tell you!'

Silence.

'Who is that jerk?' they must be thinking, or 'Pretty cheeky, that one', or, 'What a hick! Straight out of the sticks.'

By the next day, everybody knows who I am.

The Beijing Arts Institute is even more strict than the Shenyang army school, but I feel so liberated being away from my home town that I can't help stirring things up. For instance, I notice that outside of classes boys and girls routinely stay away from one another, as if pretending the opposite sex does not exist. I just don't understand! I decide to address the issue with the director and his deputy.

'Something's wrong,' I appeal to him. 'In a year from now we'll have our diplomas. Do you really think we'll be able to keep dancing together if we don't even *speak* to one another?'

One afternoon a few weeks later, exhausted from a training session, I visit the director's office again. It's unbearable being cooped up inside all day, in the middle of Beijing.

'Sir, I have an idea I would like to share with you.'

The director looks up. He's getting used to my barging in. I don't think he even minds it much – my suggestions are often good and I am a welcome distraction from his routine.

'Go ahead.'

'Don't you think that the arts education we get at the Institute should be more wide-ranging?'

'Of course. All artistic disciplines are important.'

'But we're killing ourselves with our daily training. In my opinion, it shouldn't be considered a luxury to study other disciplines.'

'Jin Xing, what exactly are you driving at?'

'Well sir, the current exhibition at the Art Museum sounds interesting. Perhaps we could visit it. Those paintings could influence our artistic sensibilities.'

My earnest tone – as serious as my thirteen years can muster – is meant to impress on him the importance of my suggestion.

The director stares at me for a moment. Then he smiles.

'But that's an excellent idea!'

I immediately run out in search of our team leader to tell him the exciting news. Though actually, I was so sure that the director's reaction would be positive (he had also taken up my suggestions for improving relations between the boys and the girls), that I had already told my classmates to get ready. Of course, the whole idea was only a pretext for getting out of classes with complete impunity.

The exhibition is deadly dull and after only ten minutes at the museum, I round up my classmates and suggest we get out of there. We take the bus back. The weather is gorgeous. The Park of Purple

Bamboos, which is close to the school, is in bloom and the air shimmers with birdsong.

'Hey!' I say. I have had a brilliant idea. 'How about a boat ride?'

Instead of heading straight for the school gates, we get off the bus right there and run down the lane to the park. For a few *yuan* you can hire a canoe and row around the lake. Everyone chips in and we have enough money left over to buy cookies and ice creams for the whole class afterwards. Fresh from the lake, full of life, we lounge happily on the grass, enjoying our impromptu picnic in the glow of the afternoon sunshine. Bliss! Needless to say, after that episode I become easily the most popular student in my year.

The following week, emboldened by the success of our expedition, I suggest we tackle a bigger issue. The woman who supervises our dorm and cafeteria is a tough, suspicious character. She spies on us every night, listening to our conversations from behind the door. She takes every opportunity to make us write self-criticisms. We absolutely *loathe* her intrusions. I often think how we could take our revenge on her and, eventually, I come up with a plan: we'll scare the living daylights out of her by kidnapping her six-year-old daughter and hiding her in a hangar. I put it to the class – they think it's a genius idea and we immediately set about planning it. We have another whip-round, three *yuan* per student this time, to buy children's books and toys. Then, we split into two groups: the first group will lure the kid into the hangar, set her up comfortably in a corner with her new toys and keep watch over her until dinnertime, at which point we will let her go. The second group will take care of the supervisor.

All goes exactly to plan. The supervisor looks for her daughter everywhere, the whole school is put on alert and our political science class is cancelled. Feigning innocence, we offer to help the distressed mother, sympathizing with her, helping her search, despair drenching our faces when we come back empty-handed – all the time secretly laughing at her distress. Then we escort her home to keep her company while she awaits news of her lost daughter. Dinner arrives and, as planned, the kid turns up, rosy-cheeked and all excited by her afternoons adventure. Her mother stands up, shaking with anger, but relieved to have her daughter back.

'Where have you been?'

The little girl innocently points at me.

'Big Brother Jin Xing hid me in the hangar!'

Wild with rage, not missing a beat, the supervisor drags me to the section director and denounces me for having taken her daughter hostage in order to cut political science class. Needless to say, I have to pull out all the stops to come up with a self-criticism worthy of my offence.

<hr />

One weekend while on leave in Shenyang, I go to the cinema with my sister. The film is a hysterically funny comedy which makes me laugh so hard tears stream from my eyes. In the dark, I hear Xianglan crying too, but hers are not tears of laughter: they are small, choked-up sobs of sadness.

I lean towards her and take her hand. It is wet with tears. 'Big Sister, we're watching a comedy and you're crying?'

She holds my hand tight and whispers, 'Jin Xing, Mother has cancer.'

We walk out of the cinema. Mother looked different since I had last seen her – she was skinnier and her hair was newly grey, even though she was only thirty-seven. But I would never have suspected cancer. Why had nobody told me anything when I was in Beijing?

'Nobody knew,' Xianglan says. 'She didn't want to say anything.'

Apparently, Mother had been to the hospital to have some tests and when her doctor got the results he asked to speak to her husband.

'My husband is away on duty. Tell me what you have to say. Don't worry, I can handle it.'

'You have cancer, madam. You must be hospitalized.'

The cancer had started in her stomach, then spread to her back. It was gravely serious. Without saying a word, my mother had simply taken the results from him and headed back home. She had no intention of going to hospital. If she was done for, well, she would prepare for her funeral in secret. She called only her closest friends to ask them to take care of Xianglan and me if the worst happened. Premier Zhou Enlai had died of cancer, and she wasn't about to turn her own death into an affair of state. Meanwhile, the oncologist, worried at not hearing anything, had contacted my mother's work unit. That's how everyone found out – including my father who rushed back from Dalian, where he was currently stationed.

Xianglan then tells me about a clinic in the province of Henan which offers traditional Chinese cures and treatments for cancer. Patients must drink a decoction of plant stems picked in the mountains, on which poisonous snakes have crawled. They call that treating evil with evil.

'And that's where Mother wants to go to be taken care of?'

'Yes.'

I struggle to gather my thoughts, to find a way to accept her choice. Why would she favour that over all the cutting-edge medicines and first-rate equipment offered by the hospital? But our mother truly believes in traditional medicine and, besides, one thing she definitely does not lack is courage. I am overwhelmed with anguish. Mother is our lifebuoy, the anchor that holds us safe and gives us courage. To know she is in danger is unbearable.

Others' reactions, though, are less sympathetic. As soon as my father's family hear the news, for example, they introduce him to a young woman whom they think would make a good match for him. Better to be prepared and not waste any time, right? It's appalling! My mother is still alive and fighting for that life, and they are already marrying off my father to another woman. I knew that they never liked my mother, that they consider her lower class and unworthy of him. But this is scandalous and, for me, unforgivable. As for my father, I have no idea how he feels about their suggestion. He says nothing. And when I go back to Shenyang to say goodbye to my mother before she sets off for the clinic, my father, the perfect Marxist–Leninist, remains silent. He simply stands stiffly, on his own, as if on duty and afraid of losing his military dignity. The ties that have bound my mother and father through their life together have probably already started to unravel, and he must feel it. Yet for all his muteness, and despite the distance that is growing between them, my father still accompanies her to the health centre in Henan. He is still at her side.

Most patients faint in fear and revulsion when they take their first sip of the Henan clinic's special potion. Some flee before even putting their lips to it. But Mother is afraid of nothing: she's done for anyway, nothing to lose, she might as well take the risk. She swallows it in one gulp and waits for divine judgement. Nothing. The decoction goes down without a problem. She decides to stay on and follow the treatment. Every day for the next three months she swallows this juice made of poisoned plants. Not only does it not poison her, it does not have any side effects either. In fact, by the time she goes back home, her health even seems to have improved.

I rarely see my mother during this period, for the journey from Beijing to Shenyang is very long and I am not entitled to many leaves of absence. The pranks of the first few years are a distant memory now; the rigorous training doesn't leave us any free time or energy for that kind of thing. But my talents as a dancer are finally being recognized, in particular in folk and acrobatic dance. For the end-of-year diploma I prepare a solo, which had once been performed to great acclaim by a famous dancer from the minorities' troupe. It is called 'Spotted Deer' and I am very proud of it. It depicts a tender young deer in a forest enjoying the sun, the grass, and the surroundings while all the time remaining acutely alert to danger. It is the perfect dance for me. It seems to express so much about how I am feeling – about my discovery of my sexuality, my love of life and my fear of both. In spite of giving a good performance, I am only awarded an intermediary diploma, since I have not completed the last two years required for the high school degree.

Before going back to Manchuria I visit my mother, who is convalescing in Beidaihe, a seaside resort favoured by high-ranking government officials, in the province of Hebei on the Gulf of Bohai. In Shenyang she had been practising *qigong*, a very gentle, traditional style of gymnastics, which has been found to aid recovery from certain illnesses, and her health is indeed improving. But she is sad. She speaks very little and her dull smile only reveals the extreme melancholy she tries to hide so as not to upset or frighten me. To cheer her up during my few days' stay by the sea, I ask her to come to the beach and teach me how to swim. I have never learnt and she is a very good swimmer, so it seems like a good opportunity. The gulf is gorgeous and the time we spend together there seems to be the one thing that brings her a little joy.

It's pouring with rain, but I don't want to waste even one moment of my stay and so I suggest we go to the beach anyway. At first my mother refuses because the wind is lifting the sea in foamy waves which crash on the sand in angry fringes. But I am so insistent that she gives in and asks the lifeguard to look after me. Floundering around like a puppy in the shallows, I look back up the beach and see my mother's frail silhouette profiled against the sand, holding her umbrella over her head, her lips pursed, straight-backed beneath a torrential downpour. She looks so alone, abandoned, like a piece of jetsam washed ashore. She looks unloved. But what love does my father give her, I wonder, living so far away? He gave her two children, but love? Perhaps he is not capable of love.

The next day the sky has cleared to a brilliant, cloudless blue and I decide to take a walk along the shore. I want to enjoy my last few days before returning to Beijing. On my way back I catch sight of my mother through a window of the convalescent home. She is talking to an older man, another patient, who looks like a government official. They seem to be sharing confidences. When I get closer I see that she is crying, and he takes her in his arms and tries to comfort her. I'm shocked: my mother hardly ever cries, especially not in front of men! I have never seen my mother shed even a single tear in front of my father. But she abandons herself into this man's arms. My God, how much love she needs… I sense that this man is attracted to her, and that she too is interested in him. I pretend not to see them and continue my walk. But I am troubled by this new vulnerability I have accidentally seen. My father is a very handsome man whereas my mother is physically rather plain; she has a trim body but her face is not exactly pretty. She's a capable Korean woman who is raising her three children (my sister and I and a little girl she later adopted) practically single-handedly and runs her family with an iron fist. I cannot equate this image with the couple I spied embracing in the window.

That scene haunts me for a long time, because of what it reveals of my mother's weakness, her secret yearning. And when, a few years later, there is talk of divorce, I tell myself that if my mother were ever to take a lover – if her upbringing and traditional values will allow her to – I wouldn't hold it against her; I would even *want* her to, just as I, too, would want to have a man in my own life.

───◦

I have a difficult time when I return to Shenyang, aged seventeen. Although the head of the regional army congratulates me on my artistic progress, I still don't get the leading roles I so crave. For a whole year I suffer from a deep depression about my constantly thwarted ambitions. Until, one day, my benefactor Song Zhaokun invites me to enter the Students' Cup, one of China's most prestigious national competitions.

Ever since my enrolment in the army school, my mother has been stingy with her compliments. The best she ever offered after seeing one of my performances was a grudging admittance that I had danced such and such a solo better than the other students. I have to be sick, in bed quivering with a fever, for her to confess, as she sits by my side and applies a hot poultice to my chest, 'Yes, Jin Xing, you were great, truly brilliant.' And then I suspect she just thinks that her appeasing words will get me back on my feet faster.

So imagine my surprise when, a few months before I am due in Beijing for the Students' Cup, she takes me aside.

'Jin Xing, if you are going to take part in the competition I want you to try very hard for first place. You are capable of it. In this world, you see, there is no point coming second.'

I look at her, astonished. It is the first time she has spoken to me like this, revealed her belief in me as a dancer, her ambition for my career. I can't get over it – is it her illness that has changed her? Is she finally accepting my artistic career? Whatever the reason, her words of encouragement give me wings. During the three months leading up to the competition, I am more disciplined than ever with my training. I make a secret pact with myself: 'Jin Xing, it's now or never. If you don't make it to the top step on the winners' podium, you quit dancing'.

My solo is called 'The Pamir Pastorale'. It has been created especially for me by a couple of choreographers who drew their inspiration from the folk dances of Pamir – a high Central Asian plateau, bordering Tajikistan and Afghanistan, in the province of Xinjiang – where they were exiled during the Cultural Revolution. Technically, it is an excessively difficult solo: it is danced with a hoop and entirely on the tips of the toes, without pointe shoes, to an intense rhythm, for six minutes. To inspire me, the choreographers invite a Pamir dancer to give me a demonstration. His name is Wumei'er and he is brilliant. He's also very handsome and projects a breathtaking virility which seduces me instantly.

My technique is impeccable and my virtuosity so precise that I can perform any sequence of movements on the spot. But I am less confident in my ability to project the same manliness as the handsome Wumei'er. I feel my height is a tremendous disadvantage. If only they would let me dance a girl's solo, I think to myself, then I wouldn't have to worry about these problems. Even my teachers have their doubts; and so a make-up artist glues a moustache above my upper lip and paints hairs on my chest to make my performance more credible. As soon as I step onto the stage, my teachers – the cowards! – sneak out to the wings. Better not to be in the audience if I screw up.

My only mistake is to tilt the hoop slightly sideways; I feel it at the very instant I slide my fingers to let it spin – a tiny lapse and shift that drops a single grain of sand into the otherwise perfectly oiled mechanics of my performance, although I pick up my phrasing smoothly and with confidence. My error must have been invisible to the audience, but the jury could not have missed it. That barely perceptible shift in rhythm could cost me the gold medal. I chew my fists in rage while awaiting the results backstage. When the time comes, I gingerly pull back the curtain to read the judges' notations, my heart in my mouth... In spite of losing a quarter of a point for the solo, I am first overall! My teachers reappear magically to receive the accolades.

Winning first prize in the Students' Cup is my first victory and I relish every single moment. It is so important to me that my talent has finally been recognized. But as Wang Guangmei, the widow of former president Liu Shaoqi, gives me the medal, I suddenly feel my enthusiasm evaporate. What was the point of all that effort and all that discipline? Why all that pomp? The huge amphitheatre of the Great Hall of the People in Beijing is full. Everybody is looking at me – finally I have my captive audience. And all I feel is a deep void inside.

The following day, the Arts Institute recants on its previous decision and consents not only to give me a high school diploma, but also to award me a second-class mention, which is very rare in peacetime. At seventeen, I am now a senior officer and am promoted three grades. Yet still the feeling of emptiness doesn't leave me.

And then something happens. Just as I'm about to head back to Shenyang, I am called to join the troupe who will perform in Paris at the French Communist Party's *Fête de l'Humanité*. I am to travel abroad, dance on an international stage! The emptiness fades away and a new sense of destiny replaces it. I have been waiting for this moment for a long, long time.

4

Rows of black suits fill the China Airlines plane. Viewed from the back, where I sit, it looks like a funeral party en route to Paris for the burial of a high-ranking officer. The entire delegation, not only the dancers but also the musicians, who are civilians, has been ordered to wear these badly cut, country bumpkin suits. Only I stand out from the crowd. I wasn't about to wear those terrible clothes! Amid the sea of black, I shine out in a superb three-piece suit in dazzling white, bought specially for the trip, with cinched waistcoat, matching white shirt, and black-and-white striped tie. I look like a groom on the way to his wedding, or a merry partygoer eager to celebrate his new life.

We have a stopover in Dubai and, though we never leave the terminal, I feel like I'm in a different world. The display of perfumes in the duty-free shop makes me dizzy. All those brands, all those shimmering boxes, their luxurious fragrances wafting all over the airport. No doubt about it, this is a place I could never imagine in China.

At the *Fête de l'Humanité* I dance my three best solos at the North China stand: 'The Spotted Deer', 'The Pamir Pastorale' and 'The Battle Drums of Jinshan'. After the applause we sneak out to visit Paris. Not the Paris of the Eiffel Tower, the Place de la Concorde, the Louvre and the Château de Versailles, all of which are on the official itinerary for the delegation, but the streets of Paris and the city's boutiques.

The stores seem to sparkle with riches which make us dream of palaces filled with beautiful things; but of course we can't afford them. Only Tati, in the Arab neighbourhood of Barbès, offers cheap enough knick-knacks for our *yuan*. Dong Wenhua, a singer friend, devises a trick with the other girls to save a few francs: a few of them crowd into the portaloos and only pay for one. At Tati, she burrows into a sales bin full of cheap shoes and triumphantly pulls out a pair of stylish heels.

'Look how gorgeous! You could never get ones like that in China!'

At the Ibis Hotel where we are staying, we are given two cans of Coca-Cola every day. I line them up, unopened, on my dresser, so I can take them back home. The only place one can find Coke in China is in luxury hotels.

The sky is clearer in Paris, the smells different, the air purer. The Parisians look happy. They are beautiful – the men, especially – and I stare at them. In the evening, we attract everybody's attention with our sweatshirts displaying the ideograms for 'China'. I stop at newsstands to look at magazines. I've noticed that some of them sell porn magazines and, while the others chat, I stand to one side and discreetly leaf through them. You can't find anything like *that* in China. I quickly flick past the naked women and linger on the men with their erections, sculpted pecs and firm thighs. Should one of my classmates call me, I will slide the magazine under a pile of random newspapers and pretend to be absorbed in the headlines.

⌒

I am superstitious, just like my mother. She has been consulting an astrologer for ever, an old blind woman who lives in a little Manchurian village and who, she says, is never wrong. Once when I visited her, she told me that I was a Russian princess in a previous life – and a very bad dancer. One day, after an argument with my dance teacher, I ran down the stairs and broke my leg. When everyone had cooled down, my teacher made me promise to be a good dancer in my next life. The next time I visited the astrologer, who is also a palm reader, she picked up my hand, stroked its lines with the tip of her nail and said, 'You have the traveller's sign. Seven or eight lines: you will travel widely.'

The Chinese government has demanded that, to save money, we must return home by train. As our Trans-Siberian Express pulls out of the Paris suburbs, I think about the palm reader's prediction. I feel that this trip to Paris is the first of a long series of journeys and that I will come back to France one day. From the train window, the French countryside looks as clean and green as the landscape in a fairy tale. The grass is the colour of a brilliant emerald and the leaves on the trees shine as though a gardener obsessed with perfection has polished them one by one. They are nothing like the leaves on Chinese trees, which always seem to be covered with a fine layer of dust. No wonder we have a saying that 'the moon is rounder abroad than in China'.

With each turn of the wheels we draw closer to the East and my heart feels ever heavier; but the slow trip back lets me savour every stop. Passport control is carried out with such disconcerting ease at each border we cross: can it really be so simple to pass from one country to another in the West? All runs smoothly until we reach the border between East Germany and the USSR, where we learn that our visas for the USSR are on some clerk's desk back in Beijing. We are obliged to change onto a Warsaw-bound train (we have visas for Poland), where the Chinese ambassador has agreed to give us shelter while new visas are arranged. I am delighted with this mishap, which will allow us to play at being tourists just that little bit longer.

Warsaw is wonderful – Polish women and children are as beautiful as angels – but it is the USSR that really interests me, because of the Soviet ballets I watched in Changchun. Yet Moscow, when we finally reach it, is a big disappointment. To start with, Red Square is barely half the size of our Tian'anmen Square, and as for Lenin in his glass coffin... what a midget! This tiny, ordinary-looking man is the great Lenin? I had imagined him big and tall, imposing, extraordinary in every way. The next day I ask our interpreter to drive us to a bakery. As soon as we climb into his car, another vehicle sets off behind us. The KGB probably. At the bakery, a warm loaf has just come out of the oven. We want to buy it but the baker, who looks downright churlish, baulks.

'But if you eat all my bread, what are we Russians going to eat?'

The interpreter drops a fat wad of roubles on the counter and shrugs.

'What are you complaining about, comrade? I'm helping you achieve your monthly target.'

The stores are empty in Moscow. The economy is ailing and inflation is rampant. The rouble isn't worth much. Why are socialist countries so poor compared to Western countries? I have been struck by the contrast between the two worlds and it troubles me.

Lake Baikal more than compensates for Moscow's depressing scenes. The expanse of water is so huge that during the seven or eight hours the train takes to circle it, you never once see the opposite shore. So that's what they mean when they talk of the vastness of the Soviet landscape! The twilight sky is mottled with pink clouds and a silver mist hangs quietly over the glistening water, which stretches out all the way to the horizon. It's such a magnificent spectacle that those of us who've dozed off wake up almost instinctively. Dong Wenhua and Deng Lifang start singing the Soviet songs we have all learnt by heart. The tunes make us cry. It must have been landscapes like this that inspired their proud songs. Such immensity of scale has surely been fundamental to the vitality of Soviet art, to the Russian character and this must be why Russia, even now in its weakened state, acts with the pride of an imperial power.

Stirred by the majestic landscape and the songs, we all feel home-sick when the train crosses into Mongolia. The Gobi Desert rolls past us – an arid steppe inhabited by rare, galloping horses – and then comes the moonlit landscape of Inner Mongolia. At each border my heart shrinks a little more. I know then, with absolute certainty, that one day I will leave China.

⁓

'Seven or eight lines: you will travel widely' – the palm reader was right. One year after Paris, in 1986, we are invited to an international festival in North Korea, in honour of Kim Il-Sung's birthday. I buy myself another outfit for this trip, this time a black suit and flame-red shirt whose collar I open out over the jacket lapels. A gold-plated chain completes the look.

On our arrival in Pyongyang the plane doors open to reveal a red carpet, freshly unrolled in our honour. A hundred Koreans dressed in shimmering costumes greet us with freshly cut flowers. Their wel-come goes on so long that our cheeks start to hurt from all the pro-longed smiling.

All the delegations are staying at the Koryo, the best hotel in the capital. It comprises connected twin towers, one facing east, the other facing west. As we pile off the buses, we are told to split into two long lines: nationals of socialist countries are directed to the east tower, and nationals of capitalist countries to the west. Even on trips, we are kept safely apart, probably for fear that any experience of Western ways would corrupt or taint us!

North Korea is a late developer, economically speaking compared to China, and yet Pyongyang is sparkling clean and the city's transportation system is a model of efficiency. There is not a scrap of wastepaper on the street, nor a car that doesn't shine as though it has been polished that very morning. The buses run continuously, so there's no pushing and shoving at stops and no need to stand during your ride, and subways allow pedestrians to cross main roads without interrupting the flow of traffic. However, the stores are as short of merchandise as those in Moscow: a few tins of soybeans garnish the shelves and that's about it. We are told that the government distributes produce directly to the people. On the other hand, the arts are considered a priority. There are a dozen big theatres in the city and all students have to take art classes as part of their high school diploma.

On Kim Il-Sung's birthday, each citizen is given an apple and two pieces of tofu. They are happy as larks, clutching their little goodie bags, with photos of the 'Great Leader' on their chests. How can they be so sincere? It's beyond me.

The preparations for the show are top-secret – which doesn't stop me from slipping backstage in the afternoon and discreetly lifting up the curtain to have a peek. Half the seats have been removed from the middle of the auditorium and replaced by a complicated mechanism which, at the push of a button, brings up a dais covered with a carpet embroidered with hibiscus flowers. A huge throne sits in the middle of this dais, flanked by five smaller armchairs. Kim Il-Sung will take his place here in a few hours.

On the opening night of the festival, a Korean troupe performs *Song of Glory* before the entire international delegation – over five thousand artists. The show is amazingly beautiful. Tears run down the chorus singers' cheeks. I wonder if it is really possible to be so devoted to a political leader, but nevertheless I feel immensely proud to be one of them. I too hail from this country. The same blood flows in my veins. At the end of the closing ceremony, the Minister of Culture invites me to move to North Korea.

'No Korean dancer can match you technically,' he tells me. 'And after all, although you have Chinese citizenship, you are originally from Korea; you belong to our country.'

He senses my hesitation and continues.

'We could make you a Merit Artist and in two years you could move on to become one of the prestigious People's Artists.' He glances at my slim-cut black suit and flamboyant shirt lapels. He must guess that I wouldn't be immune to this kind of flattery. I look away.

Two days earlier we had attended a wonderful show presented by children from Pyongyang Youth Palace. The youngest performer was seven, the oldest fourteen or fifteen. The children were in charge of everything, including production, lighting and sound. It had made me think that, in spite of its poverty, Korea had succeeded in producing artists of great talent . It had made me proud. And now this minister – North Korea's Minister of Culture no less – was offering me the chance to join them in that extraordinary enterprise.

He is eager for my reply, going on:

'You'll be treated like a minister: government car, large apartment...'

It is so tempting. But I think about the freedom that I sensed in Paris; about the Coca-Cola cans all lined up on the dresser of the Ibis Hotel, which I handed out to my parents and colleagues when I returned to China; I remember Dong Wenhua's laughter at Tati and the erotic photos which had made my heart beat so fast. That's the life I want, but I can't admit it. Instead I come up with an excuse to buy myself some time. 'I'll have to ask my mother.' I am only nineteen, after all.

The minister nods. Perhaps he is not fooled by my answer.

There is a club on the ground floor of the hotel where foreign visitors are entertained in the evenings. It is out of bounds to us working artists from a communist country, but that doesn't stop Liu Shikun and Dong Wenhua from sticking their noses around my door and announcing, 'We're on our way to the club, Jin Xing. Want to come with us?'

'We're not allowed, you know that.'

'Oh please! To hell with that. Come on, come with us. We'll just hit the dance floor and then come back.'

The club is thick with people and smoke. We thread our way through the dancers, discreet and invisible. Everything's OK. We go back to our rooms. Nobody has seen us.

At breakfast the next day, the troupe's vice-president strolls over to our table and sits down opposite me.

'Jin Xing, where did you go last night?'

I exchange looks with Liu Shikun. Dong Wenhua dips her nose in her bowl. We're done for. Those people have eyes and ears everywhere! No point in lying.

'We went down to have a drink and a dance.'

'To the club?'

'Well… yes. They've got great music there, you know.'

The vice-president looks like he's got a bone stuck in his throat. The other two keep their mouths shut and throw me anxious looks. How on earth am I going to get them out of this jam?

'Were there any Third World people there?'

'It was literally crawling with them!'

Liu Shikun bursts out laughing.

The vice-president doesn't laugh exactly, but a shadow of a smile hovers around his lips.

'Very well.'

Without a muscle moving in his face, he gets up, nods farewell and walks off.

The three of us exchange another look, but this time we're trying to stifle a giggle behind the vice-president's back. He knows perfectly well that Dong Wenhua – the famous singer – and Liu Shikun – the leading artist – were with me. How can he slam me with a self-criticism without compromising them?

That evening we board the night train to Kimchaek, a city on the Japan Sea, where we are going to perform two shows. Our guide is originally from Kimchaek, and she has brought her daughter with her. When I take out a chocolate bar from my bag and share it with Liu Shikun, the little girl stares at us. Or rather, she stares at the chocolate, with eyes as big as saucers.

'You want some?'

She doesn't say anything, but continues to stare at me. I hand her a piece. She doesn't dare take it. She looks as if she has no idea what it is. I try out my pidgin Korean.

'Eat. Delicious.'

I bite into my piece to show her. She tastes it gingerly then wolfs down the rest of the bar, which is soon smeared all over her face.

'Stop it!' her mother says, trying to grab the bar from her, but the little girl fights back. It's not that our guide is shocked by the way her daughter is stuffing her face; rather, she wants her share of it.

'Don't eat it all! I've never tasted it either. Let me have a little!'

It's horrible to witness. Pyongyang's pretty, smiling face seems to hide a great deal of misery. The thought occurs to me that we have been put on the night train so that we don't see the poverty of the provinces as we travel. I get up and walk through all the carriages collecting chocolate bars to offer to the little girl.

Before our departure we are invited to a sumptuous banquet attended by major North Korean artists, one of them being the star of *The Flower Girl*, a classic film famous throughout China. I am so proud that I ask to be photographed by her side. But throughout the evening, with all its excess and pomp, the image of the chocolate girl keeps coming back to me. This is a country of such extremes and it makes me ill at ease. In China we have a saying: 'He who clings to his prestige will know many tribulations'. Doesn't that apply to North Korea as well? What is the point of this impressive showcase, those munificent feasts, if the population outside is starving? I do not regret having refused the Minister of Culture's offer. My people's biggest weakness, I see, is to believe that they are more powerful than they really are.

⌇

On my return to China, Mr Men invites me to choreograph a dance number in collaboration with him and a teacher from the Beijing Dance Academy. At our hotel in Beijing, he sits on my bed and pats the space next to him. I dodge him as usual, but he asks me to stop by his room later, so that we can continue our discussion. I make up an excuse. I am tired. It's late. We have to get up early for rehearsals. The next evening, I push open my door to find him waiting for me in the darkness of the bedroom. He presses me against the wall. I push him away.

'You are a very attractive boy, Jin Xing. Not only a talented dancer.'

He strokes my hand. I tell him he is my teacher, that I admire and respect him enormously, but that he is my father's age and this is not appropriate. I don't want to sully our teacher–student relationship with ties that would undermine it, blah, blah, blah. I do my utmost to make sure he doesn't lose face. He acquiesces and leaves me alone after that. To my great relief, we continue our rehearsals without problem.

The dance number I present at the National Competition at the People's Palace in Beijing is called 'When I Became a Soldier'. It isn't a solo, but an ensemble piece, which I lead as principal dancer. Traditionally, only solos win prizes at the National Competition. My friend Liu Qian is prima ballerina in another ensemble, and together we win the jury's special prize. It is a great honour, and I should feel well satisfied. But instead I am overwhelmed by the emptiness I felt after winning the Students' Cup. The difference this time, though, is that I now know what I am searching for.

'I've just come back from a work trip to the United States,' Mr Men tells me a few weeks later, when I get back to Shenyang. 'I was there with Yang Meiqi, the director of Guangdong Dance Academy. I believe you know her. She was on the Students' Cup jury.'

I nod. Of course I know her. What is he driving at?

'I thought about you, Jin Xing.'

'Why?'

'The Americans dance in a much freer style than we do. They call it modern dance. I think you would be interested.'

I nod to encourage him to go on.

'We have just signed a cultural exchange project with the Americans. The Asian Cultural Council and the American Dance Festival are to run the first ever modern dance class in China. It will be an experimental class, taught by American instructors.'

I stare at him, holding my breath. He stops, and then resumes, as if he had forgotten an insignificant detail.

'Oh, and at the end of the school year, the best student will be selected to continue his studies in America.'

America! That's Paris times ten, times a hundred, times a hundred thousand even! Cans of Coke multiply before my eyes. They appear dancing arabesques, fizzing over with the pressure of millions of trapped bubbles. But my expression remains neutral. There is something in Mr Men's tone that makes me wary and reminds me of how manipulative he can be. What new game is he playing now? I don't trust him, not after all those years of dancing the cat-and-mouse minuet with him. Today is certainly not the day to open up to him. We both know perfectly well that I am a soldier and that the army will never let me go. It's merely a spell to reel me in, a spell which will disappear as soon as he has me in his power. Now you see it now you don't.

'Really?' I say. 'And where will that class take place?'

'In Guangzhou.'

Guangzhou! The Guangdong Dance Academy in Guangzhou is the lowest-ranking school in the country. No self-respecting dancer would agree to set foot in there. Anyway, with my background in Russian ballet and Chinese acrobatics I don't have the foggiest idea what 'modern dance' is. Never mind. Having endured the superhuman stretches at the Arts Institute, I am willing to take up any new discipline if that's the price of escape. Besides, I have heard about these clubs in New York where men can meet freely; men that westerners call 'gay'.

Mr Men's eyes are on me, like those of an eagle watching his prey, waiting for my reaction. I don't say anything.

A few days later, while we're in the middle of a rehearsal, Yang Meiqi slips into the studio and observes us. At break-time, I nonchalantly ask her what she is doing up here in Manchuria. She happens to be selecting students for the new modern dance class in Guangzhou, she says. I feign surprise and, jumping at the chance, ask her to register me for the audition.

'You don't need to pass an audition. I'll take you. But do you really think the army will let you go?'

That is Mr Men's question exactly when I ask his permission later that day, but his tone is markedly more cutting.

'So you really think the army is going to let you go?'

'You're the one who told me about it.'

'You have completed your studies. You just won the jury's special prize at the National Competition. It's unthinkable for you to even consider leaving just when you will finally be of service to the army.'

'It's a unique opportunity for me. It's only for one year and it will increase my knowledge and broaden my technique.'

A mask of fury grips Mr Men's face. I see in his eyes the same irritation, and the same determination to thwart me, that I have seen before when I refuse his passes. So *this* is still the problem. His wounded pride. He holds a grudge. He wants to hold me in his power. But I am no longer at his mercy like I used to be. I am the PLA's star dancer, two-times winner of national competitions. My position is much stronger. This time I won't let myself be intimidated and I won't try so hard to save face on his behalf. This time I will be clear and direct.

'Mr Men, my feelings towards you are those of a student towards his teacher. I respect you but that is all. You are older than my father. It is out of the question for me to sleep with you.'

Touché! In a flash, he is equanimity itself. He tips back his chair.

'I don't know what you're talking about. You have misunderstood me. I am simply trying to protect your talent and your training. There's no hidden agenda, but you must fulfil your obligations to the army.'

'I don't believe you. If you were concerned about my future, you would encourage me. Let me go to Guangzhou.'

'Guangzhou! That school is worthless and you know it.'

'I'll get there somehow.'

'Not without my permission you won't. I am your boss, I am the one who gives the orders, and if you persist in this vein you won't be dancing here any more either. No more solos. You won't even get onstage.'

His attack is strong – but I'm ready. I fling my final grenade, and this time I remember to pull the pin.

'Mr Men, do you remember that evening in the hotel in Beijing a few months ago, when you came to my room? You made me a proposition… that you shouldn't have made. Well, I taped our conversation. If you don't let me go, I will denounce you to the Director of Cultural Services.'

It's all bluff, of course. I didn't record a thing. He chuckles with contempt and gets up.

'So you're threatening me, you little crook! You're a fool. I am the director of the troupe. Who do you think they'll believe: you, or me? Just drop it!'

The next day I ask the Director of Cultural Services for some time. He is a general, one grade above Mr Men. I tell him, straight-forwardly, that I am tired of fending off Mr Men's advances and that I want to take the modern dance classes at the Guangdong Dance Academy, but that Mr Men won't allow me to go.

The director looks distressed. It is not the first time Mr Men has done this. He is sympathetic, but keen for me to understand that he is a choreographer of immense talent and that the army can not risk losing him. On the other hand, he acknowledges that I myself am an award-winning dancer and the army must recognize my talent and help develop it…

He weighs the pros and cons. He wrings his hands. And, finally, he comes up with a solution.

'Listen Jin Xing, this is what we'll do. The army will send you to Guangzhou for a year. And at the end of the year you'll come back.'

'Fine,' I say. 'One year, then I come back.'

'On one condition: you participate in the end-of-year show before leaving.'

The end-of-year show is *The Eagle of the Northern Border*, in which I am due to dance the principal role. I agree to his caveat, but I have one of my own: I want my plane ticket to be in my hands before the show, otherwise the deal is off and I don't dance.

He hesitates, an imperceptible pause, before brushing off my request with a nonchalant flip of his hand.

'We'll talk about it.'

When I ask him about the plane ticket one week before the show, I get the same vague response. I have played fair and attended all the rehearsals, but they have not been true to their word. 'If that's the way they want to play it,' I decide, 'then fine. I will just have to show them what happens when people try to push me around.'

I stop eating, stop rehearsing, and refuse to dance my solo. The choreographers urge me to eat something. But I won't budge until I get my ticket. The same strategy worked on my parents when I was nine years old and I know I can make it work again now. But this time, I'm more prepared. There'll be no starvation – I eat chocolate on the sly.

Two days later I have my plane ticket.

5

Modern dance. I don't have a clue what it's all about and nor, apparently, do the other students, who are all fresh from the boondocks. I don't care. I am in Guangzhou to get the American fellowship and after observing the other dancers, I am convinced I have a good chance of winning it. There's no way I'm letting anyone steal it from under my nose.

What I hadn't expected, and what comes as a great surprise in my first classes at the Guangdong Dance Academy, is that freedom of expression is not only allowed but *encouraged* by the American teachers. In traditional Chinese dance, emotions are codified and exaggerated – one 'plays' anger, happiness, or sadness without connecting it to the actual dancing. Anyway, military dance is essentially just propaganda: we personify valiant, warlike soldiers to inspire the troops. There can be no room for human sensibilities. In modern dance, however, emotion is articulated through movement. It's expressed organically, and face and body are in harmony. It is a revelation to discover this, a whole new form.

At first, none of my American teachers in Guangzhou are aware that I am in the army. I am just one of their best students, nothing more. But one Sunday afternoon, while walking in the botanical gardens, I decide to tell one of my favourite teachers, Sarah Stackhouse, a dancer and choreographer with the Limón Dance Company. Instead of going out in jacket and trousers like the rest of my classmates, I show up in the full uniform of the People's Liberation Army – complete with regulation cap emblazoned with the red star.

Strolling down the peony-lined path, I feel pretty sharp. My classmates applaud and giggle. But when she sees me, Sarah Stackhouse turns livid. She looks as if she's just been given bad news. She leans towards our ever-present interpreter, who translates, 'Why are you wearing army uniform?'

It so happens that in Sarah Stackhouse's class we've been rehearsing a dance from the José Limón repertoire, an anti-war piece. Maybe she thinks I'm making a comment on the relationship between dance and war.

'I am an army dancer. This is my uniform.'

I pirouette to demonstrate my virtuosity and the others applaud. OK, I am showing off, but we army dancers are known for our superior technique and I want her to realize who she's dealing with. It seems, however, that she neither appreciates my uniform, nor my enchaînements. She shakes her head and looks offended. When she speaks, her voice is shrill.

'No more uniform,' the interpreter translates.

She remains long-faced for the rest of the walk. I am vexed. I thought she'd be proud of me. Doesn't she get how prestigious it is to be a People's Liberation Army dancer? I tell myself that America is another culture and try not to feel upset.

⁓

While we're rehearsing a show we're taking to Beijing, my mother phones me unexpectedly from Shenyang.

'I am going to Beijing, Jin Xing.'

'Really? What for?'

'I have plans there.'

She has been wanting to start a business for a long time. Has she finally convinced Father to let her? Her voice seems more self-assured than usual.

'And Father?'

'He's OK. He can take care of himself.'

'No, I mean… I know he doesn't approve of your plans.'

'I don't care if he doesn't agree. We are not together any more. We got divorced.'

I don't know what to say. She takes my silence for disapproval.

'Last time we talked about that you told me you had no problem with it. Your sister is up in arms, so do me a favour and give me a break.'

'But I didn't say anything! It is just a shock to hear it. In fact, I think it's probably a good thing. You don't love each other any more. It's right that you should separate.'

I mean it. I am truly happy for her, remembering the scene I witnessed at the Beidaihe convalescent home, when she cried in the arms of that older man, she who never once cried in front of my father.

In Beijing, a man sidles up to me at the banquet that follows the dance gala and whispers, 'I loved your performance. It was very moving.' The voice is familiar. I turn around to see the star of the famous TV series *The Monkey King*, a children's fairy tale that I used to watch when I was young. He plays the part of the Monkey King's master, the wise man.

'I didn't get your name, forgive me.'

His eyes are beautiful, peaceful. He is older than me, around thirty; I am nineteen. I'm flattered by his compliments.

'You are a talented dancer,' he continues. 'May I invite you for a drink later?'

I don't even have to think about it. A famous actor inviting me to his room for a drink. My God! I race there. We drink. We chat. And then his eyes glaze over, just like Mr Men's used to, and his hand brushes my wrist. So it wasn't only my artistic talent that moved him... Well! He is the epitome of the virile actor. An icon. All the girls have a crush on him. I can't get over it.

The love of men for other men is something that is not talked about openly in China. There has always been homosexuality, but it is kept secret or disguised as friendship. What could be more normal than a friendship between two boys? My love affair with the TV star, my first love, is a very Chinese story. Ambiguous. Not even really sexual. To tell the truth, I had no idea what men do together. We touch each other. We caress each other. When he comes to visit, he sleeps in my bedroom at the Guangdong Dance Academy: he is my friend, after all. It's perfectly normal and nobody sees anything wrong in it. I find an excuse to sleep over at his place whenever I have a performance in Beijing. He is single and still lives with his parents and they too accept our friendship in all innocence. And that's all there is to our relationship. We are not 'an item' – that would be unthinkable, but I dream of love, of walking hand in hand with him like lovers do.

One day he invites me to spend a weekend in Beijing, and that evening, coming back from a show, we ride home on his bicycle – even though he is a big star, he rides his bike like everyone else. In the balmy night, with my arms wrapped around his waist as we cycle through the city, an extraordinary feeling of happiness comes over me. I rest my head against his back. If only we could spend our lives together, in each other's arms like this. Suddenly a thought flashes through my mind: if I was a woman, we could, for real. Without even thinking, I blurt it out.

'You know, maybe I could change sex, and we could stay together forever. What do you think? Hey? If I became a woman?'

Oh, God! What did I say? We lurch sideways as he makes a sudden turn, and almost topple over. He straightens up the bike just in time and looks over his shoulder. I can't see his face too well in the dark, but I can feel his fury.

'Don't ever do anything as stupid as that! Do you hear me? Never!'

'Why? That way we could be together. Otherwise, I'll never be able to be with you for real.'

He starts to push on the pedals as if heading for the finish line in a race. I've never seen him so nervous.

'You are out of your mind! How can you even think of something so ridiculous?'

I, on the other hand, feel very calm. This idea that I have never verbalized before all of a sudden strikes me as being the perfect solution. If I become a woman, then we can have a real relationship. Everyone tells me how handsome I am, and that I have fine features. I would make a pretty woman, I think. OK, I could never have children. On the other hand, there'd be no risk of an accidental pregnancy either. I change sex, and whoosh! We are a couple. A big star like him, he could help me if he really loved me. The only catch is that if he is gay and I become a woman, he won't want me any more. But that doesn't occur to me. I am naive, no doubt, but to my mind, that night, my reasoning seems watertight.

At the end of the school year, the American teachers pick me as the best candidate for the US fellowship. I have won my bet: the gates of the West are wide open. The only problem is that I don't have a passport. Soldiers don't have identity cards because we belong to the army. We can travel with the army, like when we were invited to the Paris festival, but only with a government laissez-passer.

I call up my commanding officer. I have rehearsed my speech. What an extraordinary opportunity it is to be the first Chinese person to go and study modern dance in the USA. It's only for a year. Think of the international prestige it will bring Chinese military dance. Think of the expertise and new techniques I will bring back to my country and to the PLA. It will be of benefit to Chinese dance in general, an excellent opportunity for the whole country even, blah, blah, blah…

There is silence at the other end of the line, then some throat clearing.

'Jin Xing. Don't even think about it. If we let you go to the USA, you would never come back.'

I hadn't even thought about that. There is only one solution: I must get demobilized and then obtain a residents' permit so I can be officially registered at City Hall, which will allow me to apply for a passport. But it's impossible: my commanding officers will no more agree to my demobilization than they will let me go to the United States.

⌒

It is the end of July and nearly time for the Students' Cup again. I'll never get out of it. Daily rehearsals are monotonous. I am listening to music in my room one evening when four classmates knock on my door. I am surprised to see them; they are friends of Wang Mei, my sworn enemy and rival for the fellowship. What the hell do they want? Coffee, they say. OK. I am polite, I go over to my little stove to heat some water, and wham! They start beating me up, thwacking me on the back, the cowards. I don't fight back. How could I, one against four? Eventually they tire and let go of me. I lean against the wall and they look at me, arms hanging by their sides, out of breath.

'What's the matter with you? Are you nuts?' I shriek.

'Big head! Time you were taken down a peg or two!'

I am treated better than the others, that much is true. I have my own room, for starters, and I lead the rehearsals. But none of that is my fault: it was the teacher's idea. We are studying modern dance, he announced at the beginning of the year, and we must have a modern attitude; those were his exact words. But my worst offence, of course, is to have been awarded the American fellowship.

'Beaten up for getting the fellowship? How pathetic! Everybody wants to go to America, but they chose me, OK? You'll just have to live with it.'

When she sees me all black and blue at the rehearsal next morning, Sarah Stackhouse's eyes well up. She doesn't say anything, but taps my shoulder and shakes her head. 'I'll never understand you Chinese,' translates the interpreter. She must think we're a hell of an aggressive lot. I sink into a depression. Two of my attackers get thrown out, but it doesn't change anything for me.

Yang Meiqi, my guardian angel, accompanies me to the local administrative office to beg them to give me a certificate of residence. Just a stamp, please, that's all we want; we'll take care of the change of address and the other stuff afterwards. But the city hall clerk won't hear any of it. Without demobilization papers, there'll be no stamp, and without a stamp, no passport. Back to square one.

It is time to go to Beijing for the Students' Cup. This year, modern dance is included as a new discipline, and the judges love our presentation. The applause rings around the auditorium, but I don't care; the only thing I want is a visa. Everything's screwed up; I've missed the boat. I am staying with my friend, the actor, at his parents' place, since he's still living with them, but even his attentions can't sweeten my disappointment and anger.

I should have been given my visa two months earlier. I'd been so sure of myself but now I am dragging myself through the streets of Beijing. My year at the Guangdong Dance Academy is over and I'll have to go back to Shenyang and rejoin the army. I can't accept it. I return, exhausted, to the actor's home, where he's waiting for me at the door.

'Jin Xing, the Academy called. Your papers are ready.'

'What?'

It's a miracle. Perhaps some city hall clerk who has seen me dance decided to arrange things. Or maybe Yang Meiqi finally pulled the right strings – she doesn't let on if so. I pack my bags in a hurry and rush back to Guangzhou to pick up the certificate of residence from City Hall and the passport from the police headquarters. By the end of the afternoon my American visa is glued into my brand-new passport. I am going to America!

⌒

On the plane from Hong Kong to Seattle I can't stop shaking. My departure was clandestine; the army do not yet know. If my commanding officers had the slightest inkling, they would have stopped me from leaving. I imagine PLA soldiers waiting for me at passport control when I arrive, their khaki red-star caps hovering behind the crowds of passengers. But all I find at the airport in Seattle is a nice Korean couple who take pity on my total lack of English (I can't even read the alphabet) and escort me all the way to the boarding gate for New York. I must look quite something: a diminutive Chinese man just 1.68 metres tall and weighing no more than 60 kilos, dressed in cool Beijing threads and a bootlace tie with jade trimmings. There are some double-takes, for sure! 'Beautiful! Beautiful!' some passersby say. 'They like your tie,' the Koreans tell me, and I relax a little. No red stars on the horizon. As our plane approaches New York, my worries resurface – they may have missed me in Seattle, but they're going to catch me at JFK for sure. But no, there's no sign of a khaki uniform at the airport, only a card with my name written in ideograms brandished by a tall, black, uniformed driver. He leads me out to a stretch-limousine parked at the curb, equipped with a leather couch, a fully stocked bar, a fridge and a TV. A luxurious den. That's the kind of car I want to have one day. My God, I marvel, and for the first time begin to wonder what sort of life is awaiting me here in America…

My hotel is on Madison Avenue, not far from Rockefeller Center. With all the excitement, not to mention the thirteen hours' time difference, I don't sleep a wink that night. By five in the morning, I can't stand it any longer so I go out. A sulphurous glow hangs over deserted avenues. At about six, the sky above the skyscrapers lightens and the streets start to come alive; at seven, crowds start to surge through the streets. I weave between the office workers, feeling invisible. I keep wanting to shout, 'Look at me, I'm not like you, don't you see? I am Chinese! I just landed! Won't you look at me?' But nobody bats an eyelid. The anonymity disturbs and intoxicates me at the same time.

Every night for weeks, I dream that the red-star officers find me, handcuff me and drag me back home. But nothing happens. I must be too small a fish to be worth creating a diplomatic incident over, and America is such a long way away. Or maybe Yang Meiqi has convinced them I will be a good ambassador for China.

CRYING DRAGON

1

My father is a traditional man, a military officer to his very finger-tips. We have never been close, and now that he and Mother have separated we've grown even further apart. I shudder to recall our walks in Shenyang, when he would march ahead, stiff-necked and with his arms crossed behind his back, while my sister and I lagged behind, so intimidated that we barely dared talk to him. But as I lie in hospital after my breast-enhancement surgery, I decide I need to tell him about my new incarnation. I brush my hand against my nipples under the hospital sheet: my first womanly gesture. Mother thinks I shouldn't tell him. Why bother? It doesn't matter whether he knows or not. But he is my father. He must be told. I have been wanting to call him for a few days now. Not only to share the news with him that his only son – the only male in an entire generation of our extended family (his brothers and sisters only have daughters), the one whose sole duty it is to pass on the family name – is about to become a woman, but also because I need his help. Now that Mother has moved to Beijing, he is the only one in the family who still lives in Shenyang, where I am officially resident, and the only one who can help me change my identity card.

If I do not change the gender on my identity card, I will not legally be a woman – and that's out of the question. At this stage, the silicone breasts can still be removed: take them off and I'll be flat as a pancake again. But it will be a different case once the major operation has taken place – they're not going to reattach a penis! I want things to be clear and official before I take the final plunge.

At first Father does not understand what I am doing in the plastic surgery hospital. Did I suffer some burns? I don't say anything. I am wearing a big, shapeless sweater over my hospital pyjamas. He sits on the couch across from the bed and pulls a cigarette out of its case. I wait until he lights up, and then I dive in.

'I have something important to tell you.'

He exhales the smoke through his nostrils in two long columns and waits for me to go on.

'Your son is going to become your daughter...'

'What?'

'...Father, I am going to have an operation to change sex.'

His face, not particularly expressive at the best of times, freezes in surprise.

'Why?'

'Because I want to become a woman.'

He smokes in silence. I watch him from my bed, my hands flat on the sheet. There's no way he can see my chest under the big sweater. He drags on the cigarette once or twice without saying anything and shakes his head a few times.

'Wow!' is what he eventually manages. 'That's big. When did you decide to do this?'

'I've been thinking about it for a long time.'

'Did the idea come from someone in the West?'

'No, it's my own idea; I've been thinking about it ever since I was little. And since I've come back to China I've been sure.'

Last toke. Last spiral of smoke. Fag-end squashed in the ashtray.

'You will finally be in tune with yourself.'

'What do you mean?'

'When you were a little boy, I never understood what was going on. I had a boy, but he acted like a girl. And now you've found your-self. Congratulations! What can I do for you?'

I had imagined many reactions, but not that one. I am staggered; maybe he's not as uptight as I had always thought. Or else he knows that once I've made a decision, nothing and nobody will make me change my mind. And I think he respects that. He agrees to help me change my identity card. As a military officer, he's right in with the Shenyang police and they all do favours for one another.

⸺

Consider the Adam's apple. It doesn't look like much – a bump on the neck that you would think could be planed as easily as a knot on a piece of wood – but it touches the vocal cords and if the ablation is not handled exactly right, there's a risk the voice will be damaged. Dr Yang gives me a local anaesthetic and starts to cut through the cartilage. To make sure she doesn't remove too much, she makes me cry out at regular intervals. It's a strange sensation, but not really painful. I visualize my neck slender and smooth, like a woman's. I will have a husky voice, but a feminine neck. My voice must stay as it is: I don't want to be shrill like a Chinese woman. That's not me.

Right after the surgery on my Adam's apple comes the procedure to remove my facial hair. I have the two operations back to back. The depilation will be done without anaesthetic and Dr Yang has already warned me that it will hurt. For some reason, though, I am not afraid. I almost relish the idea of suffering, as if that will be the sac-rifice I must offer in exchange for this enormous gift I am to receive. Why should I expect not to have to make a pay-off for this privilege? While the nurses prepare the needles, Dr Yang explains the pro-cedure again. Each hair follicle must be individually removed with a needle. The area around the mouth is especially sensitive and so, if anaesthetic is used, there's a risk that the lips may swell and the stitches might be wrongly positioned as a result. Therefore, it's better to operate without. She doesn't need to convince me.

'Go ahead. No anaesthetic.'

My God, what horrible pain! First, the incisions around the lips; then torture by needle as it is repeatedly jabbed into the dermis to remove each follicle. Unfortunately, for a Chinese man I am very hairy. For a wannabe woman, that is the ultimate bad luck. Somebody – I don't know who, a friend, or a nurse, I am so out of it I can't even tell – gently strokes my hand. I focus on the soothing feeling. When it comes to the stitches, I almost faint. One of the camera crew passes out. I hear the others fussing around him, trying to bring him round. This never-ending pain reminds me of the stretching sessions in the barracks, our bellowing like cows in a slaughterhouse. Still I bear it, chiefly for Dr Yang's sake. I don't want to upset her: she has got to keep it together and the nurses are not helping – from the corner of my eye I see two of them nattering near the instrument tray. They are so distracted that they pass a blunt scalpel to the doctor, who angrily rejects it. I could cry, not from the pain, but out of rage at those couldn't-give-a-damn nurses.

After four or five hours – though it could have lasted ten hours and I wouldn't have noticed, my sense of time is so shot – the torture ends. By the time they get to the final stitches I can hardly feel anything; my body must be used to the pain. A nurse leans over to admire the end result. 'Dr Yang has performed a real craftsman's job,' she says. My face looks like a piece of hand-stitched embroidery.

The photo I send to my father for my new identity card shows a pretty woman with fine features, a smooth chin, a pulpy mouth and long hair parted down the middle and falling to her shoulders. No make-up. I won't allow myself any make-up until I become a complete woman. But I am happy with the result. The photo will look good on my new ID card. When he comes back from Shenyang, my father recounts his interview with the police officer.

'Mr Xing, what can I do for you?'

'It's for my son. He can't come. He is in Beijing.'

'OK. Does he need to renew his ID card?'

'Well, in a manner of speaking, yes. But it's a little more complicated. My son, you see, well, to tell you the truth, he has become my daughter.'

'Really? We've never had a case like that. In the whole history of Shenyang police headquarters, never!'

'It's a first then. Look, here is her picture.'

'She's quite a looker, your daughter.'

We laugh about it together. I am relieved. My big operation is set for April: a spring date for my rebirth. There are still a few more weeks to wait and for the time being the trees outside my hospital window remain stripped of leaves, the winter sky still the colour of lead.

—◦

The Asian Cultural Council accommodation is on 15th Street near Seventh Avenue, halfway between Chelsea and Greenwich Village. It is a tiny studio apartment, not much more than twenty square metres, but right in the heart of Manhattan. A tall blonde, Eileen, comes to pick me up and take me to the bank. I need to apply for a bank account – this is a capitalist country after all, unlike China, where we regular mortals don't dream of having such things. When I pull out my chequebook at the supermarket I feel rich (even though I need Eileen's help to write my first cheque!). And I'm so excited by all the *stuff* they sell, especially the ice creams. Ice cream! We don't have ice cream like that at home. Once I've stuck my spoon in the little tub that's it, I abandon myself, I can't help it. And the orange juice! I drink a whole carton in one sitting.

Wang Yanyuan is a Chinese soprano and, like myself, a fellow of the Asian Cultural Council. Her room is directly below mine and we become fast friends. She teaches me how to bargain hunt. Apparently, although they are rich, Americans watch their spending too. I am astounded: in a country so prosperous, the rich also economize? I come to the conclusion that countries behave just like individuals: the poor like to act flashy, whereas the well-to-do tend to be a bit stingy.

Not knowing any English is no problem in my dance classes, but it does affect my social life. Apart from my shopping trips with Wang Yanyuan, I feel very lonely. When I come back home at night I turn on the TV and watch sitcoms. I walk down to the corner bar and listen as the conversations become increasingly drunken. Little by little I start to recognize a few phrases, but I remain dumb as a carp. The ACC, which takes care of my whole life – rent and dance classes, plus a thousand dollars a month for personal expenses – eventually hires a teacher to give me private English lessons: Christopher, a gay man who speaks not a word of Chinese. I have no idea how we will communicate, but Sarah Stackhouse tells me it's the only way to learn and that I would be well advised not to hang out in Chinatown too much. There are Chinese immigrants who have lived in New York for several decades and still can't speak English. So I apply myself with Christopher, but my old, bad schoolboy habits are hard to break: I never do my homework.

⌐⌐

'Would you like me to walk you back?'

John is balding, like Lenin, and he wears little wire-framed

With my family in Shenyang during the summer of 1969.

My sister and I, 3 May 1969. We are both holding the Mao Bible. The writing says, 'Read Mao and you will belong to a new generation of revolutionaries.'

On stage with the army kindergarten, 1 June 1974.

A shooting lesson in Manchuria, 1979. I was being trained as a dancer, but I was also a common soldier.

With my sister and my cousin in Shenyang, 1975.

This picture was taken in one of the army dance studios. I am practicing a classical Chinese dance. Shenyang, 1983.

At the age of twenty I was already determined to be one of the greatest dancers China had ever known.

In front of the Versailles palace in Paris during my first ever trip abroad, 1985.

In the leather goods shop in New York's Greenwich Village, where I worked part-time during 1990. My life at that time was a patchwork of odd-jobs, training and dance classes.

With my dog Lulu in New York, 1991.

glasses. Not my type at all. He speaks fluent Chinese however and, at the Chinese party to which we were both invited, he doesn't leave my side all evening. In the subway he suggests we go to Greenwich Village. Later, after a tour of the bars, he invites me to his place for a nightcap. As it happens, he lives right next door. His place is tiny and its two rooms so full of books that the bed feels like it is at the bottom of a book-lined well – I have never seen so many in my life, outside of a bookshop! He rambles on at me about his experiences in China, and asks me lots of questions. I enjoy speaking Chinese with him, but I am getting weary.

'You can sleep here, if you like.'

Once again, *that's* what this was all about. How naive can I be? I'm not really attracted to him – I like big, tall, virile men – but I am curious. Western sexuality! It is the stuff of legends and I finally have the chance to experience it for myself. At least he lives up to Westerners' reputations on that score.

He touches me from behind.

'May I?'

I sit up abruptly.

'Are you insane? It's not possible!'

He laughs.

'You never tried?'

'I know there are men who do that, but not me, thank you very much.'

He's not deterred. He prepares me gently.

'Let me show you how enjoyable it is.'

He laughs again at my look of horror.

'No! Absolutely not.'

I do, though, eventually let him penetrate me. And on another night after that; but no more.

Christmas is coming. The lights thread through the trees with a thousand twinkles, the majestic fir rises like a giant between the Rockefeller Center towers, and the department store windows display animated scenes from fairy tales. I take photos to show people back in China what an American Christmas is like. I have bought a pair of calfskin boots, trendy leather trousers and a leather jacket, which I wear to the ACC Christmas party. I want to impress the Americans, show them that Chinese people aren't hicks, prove that we can be stylish too.

Christmas in New York is miserable if you don't have family or friends around. I have John of course, but our affair has petered out. He is a friend, not a lover. We stroll along the illuminated avenues side by side. It's cold already and night falls early. In the window of a pet store, puppies scratch the glass, maybe in the hope they will attract passers-by. Boy, I'm sad! A tiny mutt with white fur sits quietly on his sawdust bed. I ask the store manager to take him out of his cage and he hands him to me. The puppy is barely larger than my hand.

'It's a Maltese bichon.'

'How much?'

'A thousand dollars.'

'A thousand dollars! Why so much?'

'Both his parents won beauty competitions.'

John pulls me aside: it's much too expensive. This guy is a crook. But I know a thing or two about Maltese bichons: the tinier they are, the more expensive. And this one, well it's hard to imagine anything smaller. I ruffle the hair over his eyes. His snout, which is nestled into my palm, doesn't move, as if he were a stuffed animal. It's Christmas, after all. The time of year when Americans shower each other with presents.

'I'll take it.'

The manager can't get over it. A short Chinese guy straight off the boat buys this expensive dog without batting an eyelid! John looks at me as if I've lost my marbles. The manager grooms the dog carefully, brushing and perfuming him, and then puts him inside a little round box, just like the ones we use for birthday cakes in China. He shuts the lid and wraps the whole thing with a pretty red and green ribbon, which he ties in a bow. It will be my Christmas present to myself! I pull out my chequebook and make it out for the largest sum I have ever written.

In the subway I balance the box on my lap and open the lid. The person sitting next to me leans over.

'Oh, what a cute little cat!'

'It's not a cat, it's a dog,' John answers in a pinched voice. Clearly he still hasn't got over my folly.

'What are you going to call him?'

Later on, I watch my Christmas present snuffle around on the carpet in my room, just a little wriggling thing with hair as soft as the most luxurious fur coat. 'Lulu! Come here, Lulu!' He turns around and rolls over my feet. Lulu it is then, since he answers to that name. I pamper him, my little Maltese, with a wicker basket to sleep in, a winter coat, a leather lead, the best gnawing bones and tastiest food.

On Christmas Eve I have my picture taken lying on my couch on a pile of cushions, wearing my new boots and holding Lulu in my arms. I send the photo to my mother so that she can see what my life in New York looks like. It is a picture of comfort and joy, and yet I feel so lonely; the arrival of the holidays has made me realize that I have lost my bearings.

⌒

The Asian Cultural Council fellowship doesn't impose strict study conditions. I am not allowed to work, but I am free to attend auditions for the various dance companies, and to take their classes and participate as an unregistered student.

In China, I was entirely taken care of by either the army or the Dance Academy, and I never had to make any decisions. Here, I have to handle everything myself and all of a sudden there are endless choices to be made: this lover rather than that one, such and such a dance class, a dessert or a piece of fruit, one sexual orientation or another... All these options, all these limitless possibilities with their shimmering prospects – it's almost too much to bear.

I hold fast to my military discipline, my anchor point. Each morning I get up early to practise or go to classes. I buy the *Village Voice* every week to check out the auditions that are advertised. I audition with Martha Graham, Balanchine, Alvin Ailey, José Limón, Alwin Nikolais and Murray Louis, and everywhere I am welcomed with open arms. A dancer newly arrived from the People's Republic of China is a great curiosity.

At Alvin Ailey almost all the dancers are tall black men who grew up with jazz. It is a cliché, I know, but they have such a strong feeling for rhythm that for the first time in my life I don't feel up to it. I don't know anything about jazz and they impress me hugely. I hide in the last row so as not to be noticed. One day, the heavyset black teacher who runs the class with a rumbling roll of the drums points his finger at me.

'You, over there, come up front.'

'Who, me?'

'Yeah, you.'

I comply. I move through the steps, I pick up the rhythm, follow the beat of the drums. At the end of the piece I bow. Silence. Then the whole class gets up and applauds. 'Did you see that young Chinese guy? Wow! It's the first time in my life I've seen an Asian dance jazz like an African–American.'

Every night, back in my room, I offer a prayer of thanks to the Beijing Arts Institute and the Chinese army for the training they gave me. I know it is thanks to the technical grounding I received in China that I can hold my own in front of these American dancers and I dream of the day when America's doors spring open for me and the offers pile in.

There are more than eighty of us auditioning for the Paul Taylor Dance Company, which wants to hire two new dancers. Next to all the muscular, well-built bodies I look small and puny. A shrimp. But in the studio, my perspective changes – technically, they don't measure up, those gorgeous Americans. What's more, the teacher calls me to the front row for every exercise. At the end of the first try-out, half the dancers are eliminated, followed by another lot at the second try-out, and so on. I make it to the last five. Paul Taylor, who is attending the final try-out in person (accompanied by his dog) applauds my performance and cries, 'Superb! Superb!' And yet I am eliminated in the last round. While we're getting changed after the audition, one of the other failed candidates explains the hiring system. It's very simple. The two chosen dancers are graduates from the Paul Taylor dance school. It's always like that. I wonder about the logic of having auditions if they're rigged – what's the point? My illusions about America are beginning to crumble. I always thought of it as the country where the best man wins. When one of the audition judges comes to congratulate me at the door, I question him in my rudimentary English.

'Why not me?'

'We always hire our students. It's a way to attract dancers to the school.'

'Why did you keep me till the end, then? That was cruel.'

'You're so talented that we were enjoying watching you dance.'

Apparently, Paul Taylor had been told by the President of the

Asian Cultural Council that he could not hire me since I had to go back to China at the end of the year. For a brief while I had fallen for the American dream; I believed that my talent would be recognized, that I would be hired by a prestigious New York company, and that I'd stay in the United States exactly as my commanding officer had predicted. But now that dream has collapsed.

It is a huge blow but it does not stop me from attending more auditions. I know I am not going to be hired, but I still want to become familiar with each dance company's style and learn some new movements – I am going to take every last piece of knowledge and experience I can from my time here. The New York City Ballet is where I feel most at ease. It's true that the Chinese army ballet training is just as good as the American training, but there's something lacking in its modern dance classes, not technically, but to do with expression and imagination.

We are at a rehearsal with the Nikolais/Louis Dance Company. I am very proud of my technique and my strength, but even when I perform the movements accurately, Murray Louis keeps criticizing me. 'You don't know how to balance your power. You are like a well-oiled machine. Let yourself go: let the emotion through.'

I try, but I am blocked. I am constantly tense. For me dance is an explosion of energy that allows me to perform virtuoso technical feats, close to gymnastics. But Murray Louis keeps telling me to let go. He might as well ask me to abandon everything I've learnt and forget my technique.

'You've got to sublimate this power you express.'

Impossible! I am China's best dancer; it is inconceivable that I can't be the best modern dance performer as well. I can only conclude, arrogant as I am, that it is American modern dance that is somehow in the wrong. I walk the sixty blocks all the way to Chinatown to calm myself down and think things through.

Someone has given me the name of a psychic renowned within New York's Chinese community and I have just one question to put to her: 'Why is it so difficult for me to become a great modern dancer?'

In a dirty recess at the back of a Chinatown store, the psychic makes me sit on a stool, takes my hands and studies my palms. She tells me the key word of my life is 'patience' – probably because nature has given me so little! I should have been born a prince, she says – a great prince – but at the time of my reincarnation into my present life, I was so impatient to come into this world that I was born too soon. God punished me by having me born into an ordinary, lower-class family. This means that I have all the right cards in my hand, that I am blessed with innate talent, but that I will need to climb every rung of the ladder, from the bottom up to the top, before I reach the regal destiny that should be mine.

I try to put the awards I received in China, all those prizes and medals, out of my mind. I need to forget technique and let spirit and emotion shine through – I just don't seem to know how to be natural. One day, Murray Louis hands me a videotape. It's a video of his famous solo *Déjà Vu*, or rather of 'Tremblement', its second movement. He choreographed and danced it himself at the age of fifty-seven and the performance was a sensation in the United States.

'Study the second movement,' was all he said.

The tape begins to play. He stands alone on a bare stage, accompanied by a single Spanish guitar. His body barely moves; it seems only to be animated by one long, continuous shiver. It's extraordinary.

'You want me to dance it?'

He nods.

'But this dance is absolutely wrong for me. There's not so much as a leap or a pirouette! It doesn't showcase my technique!'

He laughs.

'Jin Xing, you don't need technique any more. You have more than enough already. What you need now is style.'

Is this yet another test, another lesson in how to forget my technique and let go? Every afternoon, I rehearse and imitate the posture of a fifty-seven-year-old man. After a week, I present the solo to the class. All the students applaud. Murray Louis wipes his eyes.

'My God, it's been so long. And I thought this piece was only good for the museum. I never would have thought that someone... that you could have interpreted it this way... You know, internationally acclaimed dancers, the great Nureyev for instance, have asked me for permission to perform it. But I've always said no. To all of them I've said that it isn't a dance, that it is the experience of a life. It's impossible to dance it under the age of forty. And you... how old are you?'

'Twenty-one.'

For a while, he remains lost in thought, his head inclined to one side, and then he looks at me.

'Would you like to perform it onstage?'

'I don't know if I am worthy of it.'

'I wish you would.'

Two days later we start the rehearsals.

'Imagine,' Murray Louis says, 'a man standing at a crossroads. He has neither ambition nor regret. Nor does he have any choice. He shivers. Yes, that's it. He shivers from the very bottom of his soul. Don't overload it with feelings. Try instead to express a very natural state, as if a fleeting emotion has been spun out.'

All the New York critics are there on the night of the show, enticed by the rumour that *Déjà Vu* is to be performed by a Chinese dancer. Before I go onstage, Murray Louis addresses the audience.

'It's very moving for me to introduce this piece. I thought it had become obsolete,' he says, 'until this young Chinese dancer gave it an interpretation that infused it with new life. I don't know what he has understood of it, but I know he expresses what I wanted.'

'Tremblement' starts without music. I step onto the stage in complete silence and wait there in silence. Murray turns on the soundtrack himself. The music, he has often told me, evokes blood beating in the veins. Little by little the melody rises and my body starts to move imperceptibly, and to quiver, as though the warmth of life is slowly seeping through me.

All I am aware of when my performance ends is the standing ovation, which lasts longer than the four-minute solo. Later I hear that Murray was dancing along with me, my mirror, in the wings.

The next day, *The New York Times* writes, 'A Chinese genius has resuscitated "Tremblement" to great public acclaim.' It is my first American success. Murray Louis has given me permission to interpret his work, which will have an enormous impact on my artistic life. After that, every time I travel abroad I ask if I can perform 'Tremblement'. For me this solo is the epitome of the modern dance that I am only just beginning to understand. It is a solo whose apparent simplicity makes it all the more difficult and complex. This paradox makes me think of classical Chinese, where jewels of meaning are condensed into a single ideogram.

John continues giving me English lessons. Every evening he calls up and we talk for an hour. According to him, phone conversations are even more valuable than face-to-face ones, because you can't rely on facial expressions or gestures to help you, you must depend entirely on recognizing the words. At night we go out. He takes me to the midnight screening of the cult film *The Rocky Horror Picture Show*, which has been playing at the same cinema for years. The spectators know all the dialogue by heart and join in with all the songs; some dress up in character and act out bits in the dark, even throwing rice into the audience during the wedding scene. It's crazy! The audience participation fascinates me much more than the film itself. It is with John that I discover the Village gay bars. There are bars for every taste, every walk of life and every age group: bars for eighteen to twenty-year-olds, for those in their twenties and thirties, for hipsters, yuppies, manual labourers and fetishists. It's like a supermarket.

To me, America is all about freedom and innovation. Provided you have talent and willpower, you can succeed in anything you set your mind to – the cliché of the American dream. Officially I am here to make my dancing dreams come true, but secretly I am also keen to explore my sexuality. For instance, am I homosexual? In the China of my youth, one never asked such a question. But in New York, there's a whole new world to discover, one whose credo is all about 'being yourself'. Fine – but first I have to find out what, who, my 'self' is.

After a few months, I go to gay clubs without John. Thanks to our daily conversations I speak English well enough to get by on my own, and the men show infinite patience when they try to pick me up. I go to all the clubs, including the leather clubs (the most dangerous ones) where they play porn movies and the place stinks of semen because of all the sex going on behind the screen. My friends tell me I am crazy, but I'm not scared. I want to see everything, discover everything, but I don't participate. I am afraid of Aids and anyway I am unable to have sex in the dark, without seeing my partner's face. I sit in a shadowy corner and I watch and listen. This wild, animal sexuality doesn't disgust me – on the contrary, it turns me on, but I don't understand it. In China, boys and girls don't even make love before getting married.

Uncle Charlie's is a bar for youngsters. Everyone there looks like a model, showing off their pecs and flashing their six-packs, pure show; whereas at Monster the punters are older, which I much prefer. After a certain age – thirty-five, let's say – men lose their purely physical power of seduction and become calmer, so you can have a real conversation with them. On the Upper East Side, at the corner of 59th and Second Avenue, there is a bar that 'specializes' in Asian men. Chinese men are in big demand for their small size, pretty features and submissive nature, and in this bar there is a code: if you want to pick up an Asian man, you say you're looking for rice, but if you're looking for a Caucasian man, you ask for potatoes. Of course, the first time I go there, I have no idea what that's all about. I push the door and right away an American spots me and walks over to check me out.

'Do you like rice or potatoes?'

Oh, I didn't know they served dinner in this bar!

'I love potatoes, but I eat rice every day,' I answer, in earnest.

He rolls his eyes.

'Oh, you're a mess!'

He walks away with an exaggerated swing of his hips.

I dive headlong into the gay world. I have affairs. Gay men are obsessed with sex! Most of them are looking either for a mirror image, for someone of exactly the same body type and age, or else for an opposite, as with old men and their very young lovers. Everything revolves around the sex act, but I am more interested in seduction and slow-burning desire; I'm after communication, emotion, and mutual understanding. There are beautiful gay men, but they are too egocentric and that turns me off. I am always attracted to heterosexual men.

Friends take me to see *Paris is Burning*, the documentary film about black drag queens in Harlem, and invite me to drag shows. 'You would make a gorgeous Chinese drag queen,' they say. But I have no desire to dress up as a woman. In the gay communities of New York I am a traveller in a foreign land, twice over.

⁓

Springtime in New York. On the streets of Chelsea, the trees are covered with pale buds. Sometimes, on soft May evenings, the breeze carries a hint of the ocean. I count my remaining days. Two months left; one month left. I work twice as hard, I dance for three choreographers simultaneously – it doesn't matter to me whether they are good or mediocre. What does matter is that I accumulate the maximum experience I possibly can, right up to my last day.

My return to China is planned for 1 July 1989. I have gradually been gaining recognition in the New York dance world, I have made the first steps towards exploring my sexuality, and now I have to pack up and leave? I beg the Asian Cultural Council to let me stay on for an extra year, but it is out of the question. All they can offer is a promise that, if I want to return at some point in the future, I can count on them inviting me again.

It is Wang Yanyuan who tells me about Tian'anmen Square. At least, I think it is. The news spreads like wildfire through the ACC. Nobody knows exactly what's happening, only that the army has been sent in and that the students have been shot down. Everyone is trying to get more details – who was at the demonstration, who has been arrested. Who has been killed. We all hang around the office, trying to find out more. The big news soon comes.

'Have you heard?'

'What?'

'There's a rumour that President Bush is offering Chinese students who were in the US before 4 June 1989 the right to stay four more years. And then to get a green card.'

'It's a hoax.'

'No, it's true. We're all going to get green cards.'

'You're wrong. We are allowed to stay longer. Until '94.'

'It's a trap.'

'I don't believe it.'

'I'm going back anyway.'

'Are you crazy? I'm staying.'

Most of us opt to stay, unable to refuse such a gift of fate. We are well aware that America is taking advantage of the political situation to gain new talent because, of course, our fellowships are not renewed. But so what? On the phone from Beijing, Yang Meiqi asks me if I'll be able to get by. No problem, I tell her. I'll wash dishes in a Chinese restaurant if need be. In the end, the ACC grants me another half-year fellowship.

2

The American Dance Festival takes place every summer in Durham, North Carolina. It's a very prestigious international modern dance festival, and I am invited to participate, observe the shows, take classes, and present an original piece of choreography. It will be my first work of modern dance. I am twenty-one and all the other participants are thirty-five or older, which makes me feel like an insecure young student.

The performance takes place at night, under a full moon. The soundtrack is a piece of Korean music, *Crying Dragon*, and I dance barefoot on a concrete stage in front of an audience seated on the grass. I kneel in the middle of the stage, clad entirely in white and with a white gag in my mouth, in the traditional pose and dress of a Chinese man in full mourning for his father. More than fifty female dancers wearing the traditional *qipao* – the long Chinese dress with slits up both sides – appear like spectres and swirl around me. By moonlight, the atmosphere is phantasmagoric. The spectators are moved to tears and at the end of the show the journalists ask me if the piece is meant to symbolize the events of Tian'anmen Square. But I am not a political artist. *Crying Dragon* expresses the pain of a man exiled from his native land. It's a very personal work.

In my second summer in North Carolina, the American Dance Festival poster carries a dramatic picture of me in the finale of *Crying Dragon*. I can't get over it: the image is reproduced on walls all over town and the shops sell it displayed on glasses, T-shirts and bags. My success in 'Tremblement' means that I am known all across America. My new piece of choreography is called *Cultural Exchange*. I have invited five dancers of different nationalities – from Russia, Cameroon, Mexico, Venezuela and China – to work on a piece of music that is universally known: Puccini's *Tosca*. Our main prop is a cafeteria table, upon which the dancers take it in turns to stand and perform; the idea behind the work is that their alternating variations each evoke the main theme of the piece and that we can communicate through dance, in spite of language barriers. But come performance day, the manager of the cafeteria refuses to give us the table.

'You don't understand. We absolutely need this table to perform. It's our main prop.'

The man digs in his heels, looks sullen and hunches his shoulders.

Change of tactic. 'I'll rent it from you. How much?'

A typical stubborn American, he remains inflexible. The table belongs to the cafeteria, it will not budge from there.

'I'll buy it. Name your price.'

Nothing doing.

I have to admit defeat – time is pressing and the show must go on. I find a bench on campus and haul it onto the stage. Before the curtain goes up, I warn the audience that there have been some last minute changes to the choreography, which I will communicate to my dancers by 'conducting' them as if I were conducting an orchestra. Instead of using a baton, I use a silk fan… a stroke of genius! After the performance, the festival director congratulates me – he clearly thinks that my 'role' as conductor was intended as part of the dance!

A few weeks before the American Dance Festival, in the spring of 1990, Murray Louis had invited me to tour with his company in Kentucky, Texas and San Francisco. I had jumped at the opportunity, not simply because dancing with Murray Louis is such an exceptional experience, but because it would also give me the chance to see some other parts of America. Up to then, I'd only been to New York and North Carolina.

On our last night in Dallas I decide to accompany Bruno, a French dancer who shares my hotel room, to a huge three-storey club we've heard about. Inside it looks like the American West of legend, full of cowboys wearing denim jeans and jackets, flannel shirts and leather Stetson hats. We are a long way from New York! A bottle of Coke in my hand, I follow the movements of the dancers – it is fascinating what dancing styles reveal about a particular place. To the left of the dance floor a man is sitting on top of a loudspeaker, dressed as a cowboy like the others. There's something different about him though, maybe because he is wearing glasses. He has a sensitive, quiet look. Just my type: I don't like loud macho guys. Our eyes lock, which makes me uneasy, and I turn away. A few moments later I look in his direction again, and he's still staring at me. He climbs down from his loudspeaker, uncoils his legs and stands up. My God, a giant! He must be close to two metres tall – and he's a dead ringer for Christopher Reeve in *Superman*. He makes his way towards me. I have nowhere to hide. Suddenly this colossal guy scares me, so I get up and disappear off up to the second floor. But he is fast as I am nimble and, just when I think I've given him the slip, he materializes behind me. He is easy to spot because his head sticks so high up above the crowd. I run up to the next floor. It's a game now, and again he follows me. Again, I break away and run down the stairs to my starting point, at the bar, where I order a Coke and sip it casually.

'Hi! Can I buy you a drink?'

A voice with a Texan accent so thick you'd need a sharp knife to cut it.

I turn around. It's him, of course, even taller up close.

'Sorry but I only drink Coca-Cola.'

Unflustered, he buys me another soda, hands it to me and starts a conversation. His name is Clay Griffith and he lives on a ranch. He is twenty-nine, to my twenty-two. I like him, big Clay with his relaxed style and his easy drawl. A cowboy is my ideal man: the most masculine of men. We do get American films in China, in our communist People's Republic, so we know about *Superman*, *Gone with the Wind* and westerns. And we're familiar with the Marlboro Man, whose sparkling teeth and rugged tan scoff at us from billboards in Beijing and elsewhere. But I have no idea what a *real* cowboy is, or does; only that they originated in America, or possibly Australia. So when Clay suggests that we spend the night together, I don't hesitate. A cowboy boyfriend – it's too good to be true.

We leave in his car, a big American boat of a car with mellow shock absorbers. He drives fast on the highway, explaining that he lives near Fort Worth, forty miles from Dallas. I burrow into my seat and stretch my legs out in front of me. I am in no rush. We sink into the hot night.

I can't really see what his place looks like, just that it's a huge trailer planted in the middle of nowhere. When he takes me in his arms on his huge waterbed, which wobbles every time we move, I am overcome with languor. He caresses me lovingly, taking his time to seduce me – not at all like John and his power-hammer skilfulness. Our bodies fit together, respond to each other, move to the same rhythm.

In the morning, I wake to the smell of fresh coffee. He nods his head towards the door. 'Get up and take a shower. I'll drive you back after breakfast.'

He brings me piping-hot coffee. He is tender and attentive and looks after me. And I'd thought our affair wouldn't last more than the night and that I would have to jump in a cab at dawn! Back in Dallas, we kiss for a long time in front of my hotel and exchange cards.

The phone is ringing when I get back to New York. It's him. His Texan drawl, barely comprehensible through the receiver, makes my heart beat faster.

'I want to see you again. I love you.'

I bite my lip. I feel exactly the same.

'Me too.'

Is love so simple? If only I were back on his waterbed right now, or on his porch with my bare feet buried in the red Texas dust. I lean back on my couch with Lulu in my arms, his little silky head resting gently in the palm of my hand.

'I want to come and see you in New York. Do you know, I've never been there?'

I am not surprised. Many residents of Shenyang have never set foot in Beijing.

'Do your parents know, about your homosexuality?' I ask.

'I am not gay. I had a girlfriend. I'd just broken up with her when I met you.'

What does he mean, he's not gay? Either he's playing with me or he's in denial.

'But now you're with me and, as far as I know, I am a man. So, that means…'

His voice drawls even more, like a slow caress.

'You have the body of a man, it's true, but for me you are a woman.'

I hug Lulu even tighter. Clay has no idea how those words tear me apart. They fill me with joy, because he has sensed what I hide deep inside; but they hurt me too. The reality is that I am a man after all, and we must both accept it.

I put this dilemma to the back of my mind and prepare for his arrival. My main concern is his size. At 1.98 metres he'll have to scrunch up like a pretzel in the airport cab, or else sit sideways. I rack my brain for days trying to find a solution to this problem, until I remember the limo that came to pick me up when I flew in from Hong Kong. A limo! That's what we need! My American friends tease me that I must come from Taipei or Hong Kong because I behave like a capitalist, like one of the nouveau riche. Let them jest; I couldn't care less.

Nothing is too good for Clay. I want his first stay in New York to be unforgettable. Broadway tickets, a party in my room, panoramic views from the top of the World Trade Center: we live love's young dream for a week. Even transplanted here, so far away from his ranch and away from his natural surroundings, Clay is still attractive to me. In this city where human relationships barely skim the surface and everyone tries to outdo each other, I appreciate his sincerity. He neither hides his Texan origins nor brags about them. He is straightforward and natural. With him, New York feels less stressful.

For his birthday I buy him a beautiful jacket from the Italian designer Missoni, and since I find the Hallmark birthday cards you can buy everywhere not at all worthy of my love for him, I make one by hand. On a piece of crimson velvet I stitch two intertwined hearts made of gold stars, to illustrate my Chinese name, 'Golden Star' – one containing twenty-nine stars and the other twenty-two – and put it in a silver frame.

Meeting Clay is like having a tidal wave wash through my life, cleansing, refreshing. I don't go to bars any more, I don't let pretty boys distract me, and I don't even accept a simple invitation for coffee. I walk along the street with my eyes downcast, as modest as a young girl awaiting her wedding day. I have finally found the love of my life, the love I have been dreaming of since my adolescence, the love I discovered in the Chinese and Russian films that played in the Changchun Studios in Manchuria. No point in wasting my time with vain flirtations.

I go to practice every morning, I dance, and in the evening when I come back I talk to Clay on the phone. We feed off each other in those daily chats. Weeks pass and my bewildered friends worry about me as if I'm seriously ill. For sure I will snap, they tell me. The shrinking violet who spends his evenings alone is just not me. Like a moth to a candle, I will surely be drawn back to my previous life only to singe my wings all over again.

They are not wrong. I do snap. But not the way they thought. One evening at the end of the summer of 1990 I call Clay. 'I am coming,' I say.

Has love made me take leave of my senses; I must be insane to choose this simple cowboy over my career. If I was a mediocre dancer, OK, but after the success of 'Tremblement', the accolades at the two American Dance Festivals, the reviews in *The New York Times*? It is irresponsible. Clay doesn't believe it either, until he sees me at Dallas airport surrounded by all my luggage.

We live as if on honeymoon, full of the same crazy happiness we shared during our week together in New York. But I need to work. It can't stay like this – *I* can't stay like this – doing nothing. Clay drives me out to one of the Dallas dance companies, but when I see the level of the students there I tell myself it is actually better to stay home. So I play the housewife. Every morning I prepare breakfast and then watch as Clay guns his four-wheel drive through a cloud of dust and whirling tumbleweed to the building site where he works. After he's gone, I do the laundry and other household chores before making his sandwiches, which I take out to him in his sister's car when she comes to pick me up at lunch time. On weekends he teaches me how to drive the tractor, work in the fields, milk the cows and ride the horses. He's a big kid at heart and he like his boys' toys: his four-wheel drive, his motorboat, his scuba-diving equipment and his horses.

A river flows right through the middle of his huge plot of land and disappears into the woods. There is also a lake, some cows and horses, and the decaying bodies of various cars and vans strewn around. There isn't another soul for miles in each direction. Clay has a pilot's licence and often he flies above me in his little tin can of a plane, I sit by the shore of the lake with a picnic basket and watch him. Other times we go boating on the lake, taking an oar each, and our laughter echoes across the silence. He tries his best to get me to waterski, pulling me behind his motorboat, but I nosedive again and again until in the end he lashes a tractor tyre to the boat and I sit myself on that instead, stark naked, and we take off. Much more fun! In his parents' swimming pool he teaches me to scuba-dive.

I would like to live this life till the end of my days. I am beginning to speak English with a Texan accent. At night I watch dance programmes on TV with a kind of detached curiosity, as if it's a familiar world that has vanished from my life. I have just turned off the TV one evening after watching a programme on ballet when Clay sits down on the waterbed next to me.

'Jin Xing, you've got to go back to New York.'

I am astonished by his words, almost hurt.

'Why? You're tired of me, you don't love me any more?'

'No, of course I still love you, but there was something in your eyes when you were watching TV just now. You've been watching dance programmes every day, and just a few minutes ago you had that expression... of sadness, I think. You need to get back on the stage.'

His words hit me right in the heart. They have broken down a door I have been keeping carefully locked since my arrival in Fort Worth.

'If you gave up dancing because of me, you would hold it against me. I would like you to love me for ever, not hate me to the end of your days. You've got to go back to New York.'

He takes my hands, searches my eyes. I look down. The waterbed sways gently under our weight. If I leave, it's over. How can he even suggest such a thing?

'Jin Xing, listen to me.'

'I'd rather abandon the stage for ever than leave you!'

He gently caresses my hair and takes my face between his hands.

'When you are old and you can't dance any more, you can come here and we'll grow old together.'

He gives me a tight little smile. I let myself yield to his caresses and lean against him. It's a fantasy I can kid myself into believing.

'OK. I'll go back now, but as soon as I can't stand it any more, I'll come back here.'

'You can keep the key to my house for ever.'

Back in New York we still share our day, as if we are still living together. No sooner do I wake up than the phone rings; and in the evening, before bedtime, it rings again. We cripple our finances with ruinous phone bills. A few weeks after my return, I panic. Now that my ACC fellowship has dried up, I don't have enough money to pay the rent and I don't know what to do. Clay tells me not to worry, and wires the money directly to my landlord.

It goes on like this for months. I think only of him; it's him I want to be with. I want to make love too, and I couldn't without betraying him. One day, it all becomes too much for me to bear.

'We've got to end it. It's too hard. I don't want to be with anyone else because you are my boyfriend.'

'I know. I was expecting that reaction.'

'Why didn't you say anything?'

'I didn't want to hurt you. You are so sentimental, so passionate, and you're so far from home that if I had broken up with you, you would have felt abandoned. I would have hurt you too much. I wanted you to initiate it.'

I cry in silence. He tells me he is a cowboy from the west, a country boy, and that his needs are simple. I, on the other hand, am a dancer who craves the footlights, who thrives on being the centre of attention, and those are things he cannot give me. Our lives are incompatible.

Tears roll down my cheeks. I don't even know how we end the conversation. He is right of course. But with him by my side I was at peace with myself. I remember what he would tell me. 'I don't give a damn that you are a boy. For me, you are a woman in every way. I love you the way you are.' I cling to his words.

I don't leave my room for two days. I sob, folded over on my bed, with Lulu in my arms. On the third day I get up and go to rehearsals. You can't spend your whole life in tears. I throw myself headlong into my daily practice to forget the pain.

In the subway, a man walks in front of me, a businessman, well-dressed and carrying a briefcase. As we climb the stairs to the exit, one behind the other, I suddenly recognize his perfume: it's Clay's cologne! I follow him. We walk out of the subway, along an avenue, then down a side street. I don't pay any attention to where I am. For half an hour I trail him, walking a few paces behind, my backpack on my shoulder, until we round a street corner, climb a few steps and then, without missing a beat, he turns into the lobby of a skyscraper. I don't dare pursue him any further, for fear of being noticed. For a brief moment his scent floats around me and I sit on a low wall in front of the building and burst into tears. Crowds of indifferent office-workers pass by, climb the steps to the lobby and get swallowed up by the revolving doors. Seeing those robots all dressed alike, marching towards their daily jobs, chills me. Back in Texas, Clay loads his four-wheel drive with wood he has sawed himself, or rides his mare bareback, western style, the way he taught me. His life is all planned out already. What about me, what about my own fate, what lies ahead? New York suddenly seems impenetrable, a profoundly foreign city.

⟋

Without the Asian Cultural Council fellowship, my life becomes a patchwork of little jobs around which I barely manage to squeeze in my dance class and my practice. By turns I am a babysitter (good for English practice), handbag seller, packer at a Korean wholesale grocer (I run away after two days for fear of damaging my back with the 80-kilogram bags), dishwasher, and waiter (working solo at a Chinese restaurant with fifty covers, I am so overwhelmed that I break dishes left and right, but still manage to fill my pockets with tips). I change outfits four times a day: at 9 a.m. I am in workout clothes; at noon, I don a waiter's apron for the restaurant; by 6 p.m. I'm back in dance clothes for the class I teach; and finally come 9 p.m. I dress up in suit and leather shoes for cocktails at the Asian Cultural Council.

After three months of this schedule, I quit the restaurant for a job at a leather goods store in Greenwich Village, owned by a friend of my mother's. There too I make my living by chatting about everything and nothing and looking trustworthy. The customers always buy what I suggest: a little bit of sweet-talk and it's a done deal. At least it's less tiring than waiting at tables.

I met Zhao Long while I was still at the restaurant. He attended the Guangdong Dance Academy, a couple of years after me, and is the lover of an American dance teacher who helped him get out of China and has lent him his apartment in New York. We take an immediate dislike to each other. He is older than me, almost thirty, and acts like a prima donna. He is also a master manipulator.

'In Guangzhou, they say you are selfish and obsessed with your career and that you will refuse to help me.'

Insulted by this slur on my character, I fall for his little game. As someone who has been in New York for two years and went to the same school as this non-English-speaking new arrival, there's no way I would let him fend for himself. How could I refuse him my help? So I take care of him: I register him at dance school, help him open a bank account and do all the paperwork. Every evening, he shows up at the restaurant where I work.

'Could you get me a job here?'

'As long as you don't speak a word of English, they'll never hire you as a waiter. Maybe to wash the dishes.'

'No. No way.'

He has six thousand dollars, he has free accommodation, and still he's whinging! He's driving me nuts. I can barely keep my own head above water, let alone take care of him as well.

~~~

Before I left China, my mother consulted her astrologer from Manchuria to find out what lay in store for me in the United States.

'She says you'll get married the year you turn twenty-three.'

'I'd be very surprised…'

It's my mother's dream, no doubt, but between her dream and reality…

'And you'll have a child the year you turn thirty-three.'

Crazy. Poor Mother, clinging to the hope that one day I will be married with children. Either the astrologer is losing it or else she is being unnecessarily cruel by feeding my mother's fantasies.

My classmate Eric and his girlfriend, Kimberley, stop by to see me at the leather store one day, just as I am singing the praises of a purple suede Hobo bag to a customer of a certain age.

'Can you believe how expensive the rents are?' says Kimberley, newly arrived from Philadelphia. 'Or else you've got to live out in the boroughs. It's such a pain!'

It is a long time since I left the Asian Cultural Council's accommodation. Now I live in a two-bedroom apartment, which is quite a palace in comparison to the tiny studio I had before. As I wrap the lady's purple bag in tissue paper and slide her credit card through the machine, I have an idea.

'No problem: you can come and live with me, and you and me, Kimberley, we'll get married; that way I can get my green card!'

Disconcerted, the lady almost messes up her signature. She looks at the three of us with disapproval. I hope I'm not going to miss my sale. We all start to laugh: let her think it's a joke. But the next morning, Eric calls me up.

'What you talked about yesterday, was that a joke or were you serious?'

Two days later they move into my apartment and a few days after that Kimberley and I are hugging each other on the steps of City Hall, with wedding rings on our fingers and Eric as our witness. I call my mother that very evening to let her know.

'You see, the prediction came true!'

She bursts into peals of laughter. She doesn't believe in the wedding for an instant. She has been waiting for years for me even to get a girlfriend, and she'd be happy with just that – the idea of a wife is just a joke! She tells all her friends that her son is so devoted to his career that he has no time for a girlfriend. Now I am married? Then I tell her the truth, that it's a fake marriage, just for the paperwork. She is sceptical, but it does confirm one thing for her: life in the United States really is very strange.

Actually, the arrangement turns out to be a better deal for Eric and Kimberley than it is for me. To convince the judge that our marriage is real, we must know everything about each other – parents, culinary tastes, intimate habits, make-up, lingerie and underwear, scars – and have to attend rigorous interrogation sessions. In the middle of one especially taxing inquisition, I get up and inform the judge that they can stuff their green card, and then I leave, banging the door behind me.

It would have been simpler to wait for 1994, when President Bush has promised we will automatically be given our green cards. But patience is not one of my greatest virtues. I want to be able to leave the States to tour and travel without worrying about my visa. To hell with the green card! As it turns out, I won't get it in '94 either; by then my life will have taken a whole new direction.

⁓

Chinese New Year 1991 and the elderly astrologer has a new prediction for me. My mother phones to fill me in.

'The Year of the Sheep is not auspicious, Jin Xing. You risk a trial. And don't drink too much!'

I am not a heavy drinker, so it is easy to be careful with alcohol. But a trial? I don't have a business: I sell bags at the leather store. I just don't get it. The forthcoming year is looking very good. My dance company is scheduled to go on tour to Italy at the end of March – we've already started rehearsing – and I have been invited to participate in the American Dance Festival for the third time in a row in June.

Zhao Long comes over more and more often, collapses on my couch, parks his feet on my coffee table, stays for dinner and whines about not yet having found a payed job with a dance company. In fact, he has been here for three months and he hasn't found a job of *any* kind. Nor has he learnt a word of English. He really is expecting things will simply fall right into his lap.

'We're not in China any more, buddy,' I tell him. 'New York is something else. It's every man for himself here. And be grateful you don't have to pay rent. I sweat my guts out from morning to night just to survive and pay for my dance classes. That's what America is all about.'

'I'd rather wait to be hired by a dance company.'

'If you're not careful, you're going to use up all your savings.'

He drives me crazy with his superior attitude and his pretensions. 'Sir' Zhao Long is the American teacher's pet. 'Sir' Zhao Long believes he will become a star without having to lift a finger. I am just going to have to teach him what it's really like to live in New York without a cent, not knowing if you'll even find the money to buy dinner some evenings.

An idea comes to me one evening a few days later. I'm at his place, having the same old conversation, only tonight it has made me particularly riled. When he leaves the room, I take his chequebook from among a pile of papers on the table and hide it behind the couch. Childish maybe, but I can't tolerate any more of his arrogance. It's too bad that he finds the chequebook the very next day, hardly time for him to feel the pinch. My blood is still boiling and, though I may be blinded by resentment, I am dying to teach the spoilt brat a lesson. I put my mind to formulating a brilliant stratagem. The next time I go to his place I tear a cheque from his chequebook, write it out for $5000 – his entire savings. Then, I simply forge his signature and deposit it in the bank account of one of my friends, asking him to wire the funds back to Zhao Long's account in three days' time. That should be sufficient time to freak him out and give him a major wake-up call. My friend isn't too keen at first, and finds the idea rather dubious; but I convince him that it's just the lesson

Zhao Long needs to learn. It's for his own good.

Zhao Long calls the next day, back from his bank and all shaken up.

'I don't understand. I had more than $5000 in my account.'

'It must be a mistake. Or else you've spent more money than you thought. You know, in New York money slips through your fingers like you wouldn't believe.'

'Look, Jin Xing, can I hit you for twenty bucks? I don't even have enough to buy myself something to eat.'

'Wish I could, buddy, but I'm flat broke myself.'

Oh, the panic in his voice as he realizes he has no idea what he's going to do, how he's going to pay for his classes! His veneer cracks so fast that I actually take pity on him and invite him over for dinner.

'Take it easy. I expect it's a computer error. And you can always find a part-time job in New York. How about washing dishes at my restaurant? They'll hire you. What do you say? Will you change your mind about dishwashing?'

He is shaking in his boots, consumed with despair. His shoulders slump under his T-shirt. I recognize the feeling. It was the same for me when I was nearing the date of my return to China. I slap him on the back.

'Don't worry, man. Things will work out.'

The next day I call my friend. Enough is enough, and I am sure he has learnt his lesson. I arrange for the money to be wired back to Zhao Long's account right away. When I go see Zhao Long he is still depressed. His head is in his hands and his apartment's a mess. I sit down opposite him.

'Look, Zhao Long, I owe you an explanation. Your dough will be in your account tomorrow. I set up the whole thing.'

'What?'

I tell him everything. He looks at me, jaw dropped in disbelief.

'I wanted you to understand that in America, without money, you're nothing.'

On the evening of 31 May, a few days before I am due in Durham for the next American Dance Festival, someone knocks at my door just as I am getting ready to go to rehearsal.

'Express mail.'

I open the door. Two cops ask me for my papers.

'Do you know Zhao Long?'

'Sure He's a friend of mine.'

'Don't think so. He's accusing you of having stolen money from him.'

'What? There must be a mistake.'

'Come with us.'

I change quickly and follow them to the police precinct. There, they ask me the same question: do I know Zhao Long? Again I say yes, and sign an affidavit without knowing anything about the subtleties of US law. I don't know that one should never sign anything, that my signature will land me in jail. Zhao Long! Of course, it's because of that stupid affair with the cheque! Has he gone mad? That evening I am incarcerated in a detention centre near the World Trade Center. The place is so dangerous that you have to wear handcuffs inside.

As they lead me to the cell, I rage at that bastard Zhao Long – that bastard! For three months he has eaten my food, drunk my wine and cried on my shoulder. And this is the thanks I get for it – didn't he get his stupid money back almost straight away? He knows very well I had no intention of taking it from him. The bastard wants to do me in.

The cell door opens. It's tiny, forty square metres maximum, and filled to capacity with about a hundred filthy guys pressed together like sardines in a can. But as soon as they see me, the crowd parts like the Red Sea, a regular guard of honour! I wonder what on earth has gotten into them – I doubt it is out of respect for my long hair and bright red T-shirt. The air in the cell is stifling and foul-smelling. Maybe they don't have air-conditioning in these old jails. An ancient fan hangs from the ceiling, creaking painfully as it stirs the soupy atmosphere. I stand right under it to take best advantage of the feeble draught. My neighbour leans over to me.

'Who are you? Chinese mafia?'

I burst into laughter.

'So that's why you stepped aside to let me pass!'

The next day, once the lawyer has given me a good dressing-down, I am freed on bail. I shouldn't have signed anything: there's a whole procedure to go through. I thought it was always better to cooperate with the police. I go home, take a shower, and call up Zhao Long.

'Two-faced swine! I help you, I invite you to eat with me, I offer you my wine and you... you slander me and accuse me of stealing your money! You are pathetic!'

He listens without saying anything and hangs up. Ten minutes later, someone knocks on my door. The very same cops are standing there, smirking.

'Did you just make a phone call?'

'Yes, why?'

'Zhao Long filed another complaint against you. He said you threatened him. Give me your hands, we'll need to put on the handcuffs.'

Seeing my astonishment, the other cop explains, 'Your case hasn't gone to court yet and so it's illegal to contact the plaintiff. We're taking you back in.'

So here I am back in custody. The cell is less crowded this time, with only seven or eight inmates. The van picks us up the next morning, but, tough luck, we get sadistic cops who take pleasure in making the trip last longer, stopping to buy sodas and sandwiches and hanging out with their mates at a street corner. I am so weak by the time we get to the court house that I can hardly walk. Two black inmates pull me to my feet and help me get out of the van, then turn on the cops – who beat them up with their batons. The two inmates go down. So these are the civil rights this country is famous for?

The judge carefully reads the press clippings presented by my lawyer and the representative from the Asian Cultural Council and, in spite of his frowns, seems convinced of my good intentions. He agrees to free me on 4 June. The deadline for registration at the American Dance Festival is 9 June so I still have time. It dawns on me for the first time that Zhao Long, the rat, must have plotted the whole thing to stop me from participating. But he screwed up. Friends of mine offer to bump him off – or at the very least, break his legs, but this time I hold back my anger. Zhao Long is a crook, but I would not gain anything from revenge. He is an only child and if he ends up an invalid, unable to dance, and I see him begging on a street corner, destitute because of me, I will be consumed by guilt. No, better not enter the vicious cycle of revenge. I am sure God will repay me some day. He will note my magnanimity. I shall hope the phrase 'what goes around comes around' is proved right in this case.

For the American Dance Festival, I choreograph the famous Chinese legend of Liang Shanpo and Zhu Yingtai, and set it to the music of the violin concerto I first heard at the age of thirteen at the Changchun Studios; I call it *Half-Dream*. It tells the tragic tale of a young man, Liang Shanpo, who falls in love with his classmate Zhu Yingtai, a girl who has disguised herself as a boy in order to get an education. But he cannot marry her because everyone believes she is a boy and so he dies of a broken heart. The part of Zhu Yingtai seems tailor-made for me.

I got the idea for the set while I was in jail: the central spotlight over the stage was inspired by the fan in my cell, and the metal banister symbolizes a prison gate. The company dancers wear flesh-coloured leotards and the Swedish principal dancer is dressed in crimson and has shaved her head for the part. She looks like a Buddhist nun or a young boy, and the company dancers' gender is also deliberately ambiguous. Nobody could possibly guess that the choreography took shape while I was in a trance-like state in a Manhattan lock-up. But *Half-Dream* also evokes the surreal situation in which I find myself at this point in my life: midway between East and West, midway between man and woman. *Half-Dream* wins best choreography prize at the festival and it's my sweetest revenge on Zhao Long, who is also taking part.

One hot and humid summer evening, I am at the Asian gay bar Sassafras with my friend Steve. An attractive, elegantly dressed gentleman comes over to offer us a drink. We chat a bit and the next day he calls me to invite me out to dinner. He is a Broadway producer, originally from England, and was once married to a very famous actress with whom he has a twenty-two year old son who studies theatre. The conversation is pleasant, he is very courteous, and we promise to see each other again. A few days later he invites me to a show, and to dinner again. On another evening, he takes me to his huge apartment on Park Avenue where he makes me a drink and then, after a while, picks up a newspaper and leafs through it. I follow suit. Here we are, the two of us, engrossed in magazines as if we were in a doctor's waiting-room. What does he want from me? I glance at him; he is staring at me. Suddenly, the door opens and his son walks in. A gorgeous boy. He introduces us, and they both leave the room. I overhear them next door, talking in low voices.

'Is he your new friend?' the son asks.

'He's a very good friend of mine,' the father answers.

'He's cute.'

The next time I go to the producer's apartment, the same little game plays out. He settles me down on a couch, serves me a drink, sits on a chair to my side, and we both pick up magazines. Each time I glance up, I catch him watching me.

'Your son is very handsome,' I say, to break the silence.

'Thank you.'

'He's exactly my type, you know.'

I'm trying to provoke him.

'Oh, stop it!'

But he doesn't make any attempt to seduce me. He takes me out in town, and everywhere we go looks at me as though I were a painting. A month after my first visit to his apartment, he takes me for a ride in his car.

'I have a surprise for you.'

We pull up on Fifth Avenue at the corner of 63rd Street, in a luxurious neighbourhood New Yorkers call the Gold Coast. In a beautiful pre-war building overlooking Central Park we take the lift up to the fourth floor. He opens the door. My God, we've just stepped into the pages of *Metropolitan Home*! Park view, wall-to-wall carpeting in a greyish shade of mauve, purple couch and armchairs, and matching curtains. He shows me around. The kitchen, the bathroom, everything's spotless. A pair of lavender-coloured pyjamas suspended from a coat hook floats above a pair of violet slippers. After going out with me for a month, he knows my taste. We go back into the living room and I lean against the window, looking out. The park is an oasis at our feet. He comes close but doesn't touch me.

'Do you like it?'

'It's unbelievable.'

'You can move in whenever you want.'

I turn to him. Is he losing his mind?

'I couldn't afford it.'

'But you wouldn't have to pay. I bought it for you.'

For a few seconds I am stunned with joy the likes of which I've never known. Living in this apartment would be anyone's dream – luxuriously good taste, in New York's most elegant neighbourhood; I wouldn't have any more financial worries; I could devote myself to dance; goodbye to washing dishes in the Chinese restaurant, good-bye to chatting up fussy customers, bowing and scraping just to sell a lousy calfskin bag!

Again I turn towards him, my benefactor. He's awaiting my reaction with a look that I've seen so many times: the look of an obsessive caught in a sick rapture, mesmerized by my face. No. I would become a bird in a golden cage. I would be his.

'I can't accept.'

'But why? I am not asking for anything in return.'

'We have never made love. You have never asked me to be intimate with you and you have never made a move on me. You take me to parties and shows, and I come to your place and sit on your couch while you sit in a corner and stare at me. What are we? Friends? Lovers? I need things to be clear. I want to know what I am doing. What I am to you.'

He looks at me without saying anything, in that way he has of devouring me with his eyes.

'It's lovely,' I carry on. 'I am very touched. But... no. I can't.'

He doesn't call me any more after that. I tell myself that he has been hurt by my rejection. Too bad.

It's the dog days of summer in New York and my long hair sticks to my neck. One day, walking past a barber's shop, I step inside and have it all cut off. I nearly ask them to give me a buzz cut but I stop short of that. Ah, what pleasure, when I emerge onto the street, to feel the cool breeze on my nape.

Three weeks later, the Broadway producer calls me again and invites me to a reception. He is already sitting at our table when I arrive. I slip into the chair next to him. His face contracts into an expression of intense pain.

'My God, what happened to you?'

'What do you mean?'

He touches my shoulder, my naked neck.

'Your hair... Why didn't you tell me?'

'Oh, it was so hot, I couldn't stand it any more.'

I unfold my napkin onto my lap. I am starving all of a sudden and the dinner, which has already been laid out on the table, looks delectable. A sigh of frustration escapes his lips and he shakes his head in an obvious fit of pique. I can hear anger in his voice.

'You don't understand. Your hair... To me you were like a figure in a painting, unobtainable and ambiguous. When I was with you, I could forget the world. I was able to lose myself. But, seeing you without your long hair, the illusion is gone.'

I look at him in amazement.

'Now my heart aches,' he continues, tragically.

'Excuse me, mister, but you never told me anything about your feelings and desires. How was I to know the role I played in your fantasies?'

He shakes his head again.

'You didn't understand anything.'

I get up from the table. To hell with this. It's over between us. But how can a relationship that has never existed be over?

HALF-DREAM

1

While I was at the army school I used to have this dream in which the prettiest girl in the troupe was making love to a male dancer I had a crush on. I hovered so close to them, invisible in my dream world, that I could see the girl's genitals. They looked like a tiny penis, and I would wake up feeling very disturbed. I must have been fourteen or fifteen and I had never seen a woman's genitals before. Are women really made that way? It was a question that obsessed me for a long time.

A week before my final operation, Dr Yang comes to see me in my room. It's the end of March and I've been in hospital for almost two months. She sits down beside my bed and asks, in a quiet voice, 'Jin Xing, do you really want to go all the way?'

'What do you mean?'

She picks her words carefully, but I can see she's already prepared her speech.

'We can stop here, you know. You have breasts now, and you don't have a beard any more, or an obvious Adam's apple. Outwardly, no one would be able to tell. If you wear women's clothes, you will pass as a woman. You can live like this. No one's going to take off your trousers or try and check you out.'

I sit up in my bed, outraged.

'Are you out of your mind? I would be neither man nor woman. I don't want to be one of those half-finished trannies you see in Thailand, with breasts and a dangling penis. No way. It's all or nothing.'

'Think about it.'

Dr Yang's beautiful face is tense and there is anxiety in her eyes. I understand her hesitation. Other than doing breast implants and facelifts, she has only operated on hermaphrodites. I will be her first full transsexual and she needs some encouragement.

'It's all I've thought about. I've been thinking about it for twenty years.'

'I understand, but you are taking a huge risk and I need to be sure you're sure.'

The plan for my surgical procedure comes from a medical textbook written by a Yugoslavian doctor that a friend of mine gave me while I was in Brussels. The techniques described in the book are radical for China, where sex reassignment surgery is still relatively new. Seven doctors, surgeons and interns are studying the diagrams in Dr Yang's office and together we are discussing the final details.

Instead of chopping off the penis and creating a vagina from a piece of skin taken from another part of the body, the penis is to be slit and inverted like a glove finger to create a short vagina right in front of the anus. Everything will be kept intact and the urethra will end at the clitoris, exactly as it does in women. The skin and tissue from the penis head will be used to make a clitoris and vaginal lips, and the nerve endings will be attached to the new clitoris in order to preserve the orgasm. Obviously, there will be no ejaculation, and no one knows if the experience of orgasm will be similar to a woman's, but all I care about is retaining the sensitivity. 'I don't want to have dead meat there!' I tell the doctors.

The real difficulty will be the depth of the vagina. A penis is shorter than a vagina, so what to do? The seven medics are pointing to the diagrams and discussing the options. They measure me. They speculate on the amount of skin available. They talk about the length of penises in general and Western penises in particular. They talk about the nerves they will have to graft onto the clitoris so that I can retain as much sensation as possible.

Once all the details have been settled – measurements, proportions, proper functionality – all questions answered, and as many complications as possible have been anticipated, the date is set for 5 April: Chinese All Souls' Day. Bad omen! One of the nurses stops by my bed to share her concerns with me.

'You should reconsider, Jin Xing, it's a day that could bring you bad luck.'

On the contrary, I believe it to be a lucky day. The Chinese call it *Qingming*. *Qing* means 'clean', 'clear', 'cleaning up', and *ming* means 'shiny'. An excellent omen, actually, and very pertinent.

The day before the scheduled date, Dr Yang comes to see me again and begs me to reconsider one more time.

'There's still time to call a halt.'

Again! How can she keep harping on this?

Reluctantly, she hands me a form. It is a small piece of paper, half a normal-sized page, but printed on both sides with tiny characters.

'What is it?'

'A paper for you to sign that exempts the hospital from all responsibility in case things go wrong.'

I begin to read the list of potential problems: haemorrhage; loss of urinary function; total or partial loss of sex drive and erotic sensations; vaginal dryness; painful or impossible sexual relations; severe hormonal problems; dysfunction of vital organs. Enough! I am lost no matter what! And yet, I sign. Let fate follow its course. I abandon myself into the hands of God and Dr Yang.

⁓

Nightfall in Rome. After the tourists have turned in, the city exudes a profound energy, both mysterious and wild – and very different from New York, which tends to erupt on the surface. Where America exaggerates, shows off and titillates, Rome raises questions about the meaning of art, classicism and human nature. In Rome, eyes seem to follow me everywhere and I am struck by all that I still have to learn. Before coming to Italy, I thought that classical sculptures like those produced by Michelangelo were works of the imagination. But when I see a boy sitting motionless on a low wall near the Forum, his profile outlined, perfectly straight, against the moonlight, I realize that Michelangelo was working from real life.

I have been in Rome for two months, touring with Mark Dendy's dance company, and I cannot tear myself away from the city's old town. New York has lost all appeal. The last few months there were too hard, what with breaking up with Clay and the Zhao Long incident. I don't want to leave Rome, so my agent finds me a minuscule studio near the Vatican, with a huge terrace which overlooks the whole city, and promises to get me a job. I walk around the city at night with my camera around my neck so that the *carabinieri* take me for a tourist and not a prowler.

Returning from a walk one night, I run into a French dancer I know, Sylvie, who is also looking for work in Rome, and I offer to share my studio with her – I offer her my bed, actually, since there is not enough room for two beds. She is blonde, tall and thin, and very pretty – the kind of girl Italians go crazy over. After a few days of living together, she tells me she's attracted to me, and asks me to become her lover.

'Impossible.'

'Why? Are you in love with another woman?'

'No, I like men.'

'You're gay!'

'Not at all. I am a woman like you.'

'Get out of here!'

'No, I swear.'

We are both sitting on the terrace. She looks at me with utter incomprehension. Hurt by my rejection, she lights a cigarette with shaking hands.

'Don't you see how similar we are, you and I? When we go out, I am attracted to the same men as you are, men who like women.'

She is sceptical. She smokes, pensively.

The job my agent eventually finds for me is being choreographer for adverts on the Italian TV channel Rai 1. It is simple and boring work, but it's a living. One night after rehearsals, I hear a TV presenter recording a show on a nearby set. Her voice is so magnetic that I stop by out of curiosity. She is interviewing army officers. I have a thing about uniform (unsurprisingly, considering my past) but it isn't the officers who fascinate me this time; it's the presenter. With long hair, and a shawl thrown casually over her shoulders, she is one of the most beautiful and charismatic women I have ever seen. A grip working on the set comes up to me and whispers, 'You might not know this, but before being a woman she was a man!'

I am floored. I have never seen such a gorgeous woman. She has none of those ridiculous mannerisms that some of the more egocentric TV presenters have; quite the opposite. Her voice is sensual, supremely sexy, and she is elegant and attractive. It is the first time I have been face to face with a transsexual. I have secretly been gathering information on sex reassignment surgery and I wish I could speak to her candidly about it – I have a lot of questions. But I don't dare. It would be too crude, and embarrassing for both of us.

Back at the apartment, I tell Sylvie about the encounter.

'I would like to change sex too. She makes me feel that it is possible.'

Sylvie is the first person I confide in.

'What! So that's your secret?'

She searches my face in incomprehension. I look away. Telling her has made my dream even more tangible.

By a strange coincidence, I happen to meet another transsexual just a few days later; but far from inspiring me, this second encounter upsets me considerably. At the ballet school where I regularly practise, I am offered a class teaching amateurs and professionals who wish to be introduced to modern dance and stay in shape. It will bring in some extra cash, so I agree. When I meet my students, I immediately notice that one of them looks very masculine. You can tell straight away that she used to be a man. She is tall, 1.8 metres, and has swimmer's shoulders: a regular guy, and ugly to boot! The success of the TV presenter's sex reassignment surgery had encouraged me, but this obvious failure fills me with doubts.

I undress in front of the mirror and study my face and the curves of my body front on and in profile. What if I look mannish after the operation? If I'm going to end up looking like the transsexual from dance class, forget it. But the fact of the matter is that, at 1.68 metres tall, I am very short for a man, but perfect for a woman. And my face is fine; nothing needs changing there – my features are soft and delicate. When I put make-up on for the stage I can look very feminine, even pretty. I don't go so far as dressing as a woman, but I do discreetly experiment with slightly feminine outfits. A pair of Jean Paul Gaultier cowboy boots with a little stacked heel, for instance, makes me feel like I'm wearing heels, and for the winter I buy a long, unisex-style coat that looks as good on a man as on a woman. I let my hair grow long and wear it loose on my shoulders. But that's it. I don't wear make-up. When I eventually revert to being a woman – and to me it truly will be a reversion, because in my heart and head I am already a woman – I will dress *ultra*-feminine. But for now I am still inhabiting a man's body, so I play the man's game.

In the street, men hit on me. They think I am a Chinese woman. But I have to convince myself first; if I don't, I will always be frustrated. I spend a lot of time testing it out, wondering if I can pass as a woman, if I am confident enough to pull it off. I may never be a perfect woman, I may never be extraordinarily beautiful, and I can live with that; but I don't want to be a horror.

Sylvie is the only person I have talked to about the operation. Nobody else knows. Italian women like me, which sends me into a panic: what can I tell them? A young actress sends me her photo and some steamy letters and threatens to kill herself if I don't reciprocate her love. I beg Sylvie to call her for me and tell her she's wrong about me, that she hasn't got a chance because I like men. So of course, like the others, she believes I am gay. How can I make them understand? My situation is hard to explain, and yet I am not at all confused in my own mind. I am actually increasingly confident. And I think I owe that to modern dance.

In New York, modern dance enabled me to express some of my deepest feelings and truths about myself. And yet, I have never wanted to be an American woman, except perhaps an American woman from the 1930s! Italian women are the ones who inspire me. In Italy I begin to believe that my secret dream may one day become reality, and I start to construct a picture of my ideal woman from anecdotes that I hear about Italian women. For instance, in Naples a woman doesn't go out on a Sunday if she hasn't had the time to do her hair properly. In Italy, when a woman goes out she must be, if not perfect, at least elegant, which is an ethos that I love. I hate the American habit of wearing T-shirts all the time, just because it's supposed to look more natural. Excuse me, but natural beauty is a privilege of the young. To look beautiful after you've hit twenty-five, you need to take care of yourself.

⁓

'MTV is a hundred times more exciting here than in America!'

Wow! An American voice. I turn around, surprised to hear English spoken in a gay bar in Rome – though the bar is called the Hangar, and an English band thrash around on the TV screen in the corner. He doesn't look American, with his handsome, Mediterranean face, curly brown hair and straight Roman nose; he is middle-aged, elegant, and has an irresistible smile.

'No, no. I'm Canadian,' he says when I ask.

'I would have guessed Italian, judging by your looks.'

'Originally, yes, you're right, but I've lived in Canada since I was twelve.'

He seduces me, Carlos. He is a psychiatrist and a university professor, cultivated and charming. He doesn't look gay at all – nor is he, or so he says. He's been married to a Canadian artist for fifteen years. In the hotel room we have rented for the night, he confesses.

'This is the first time I've made love to a man.'

'But I thought...'

'No. I've had massages, that's all.'

'You have no children?

'No.'

'How come?'

'I didn't want any. I had a vasectomy. I think that... I always thought I was bisexual, so children...'

I attracted a lot of men because I had long hair, which made me look androgynous.

During a performance in Rome.

I had this picture taken for the first performance of *Half Dream* in China, in 1993. *Half Dream* expresses the ambiguity I feel at heart – caught between East and West, man and woman.

This is the first picture of me as a woman, after my operation. Beijing, 1995.

Shortly before my solo in *The Rite of Spring*. A journalist wrote to the local government complaining that transsexuals should be banned from the stage. Their reply? 'Jin Xing is a serious dancer and her company gives extraordinary performances.'

During a rehearsal in Beijing, 1995.

In my bar, Half Dream, in Beijing, 1998.

Conducting a dance class for the army in Shenyang, 2001.

At home with my children Leo, Vivian and Julian in 2003.

I haven't found such sexual compatibility with a man since Clay. Carlos isn't in a rush to penetrate like most gay men; instead he caresses me sensually as if he were a tender heterosexual man touching a woman. I let myself go with him, to give him as much pleasure as he gives me. He has to fly back to Canada the following day, which makes our night all the more intense. In the morning when I wake up, he stares at me with a heavy, meaningful look and gives me his card. I return it.

'Let's leave it to chance.'

I don't want to get involved with a married man and risk destroying his marriage, but I don't want to leave him quite yet either, so I accompany him to the airport. At passport control he holds me in his arms for a long time.

A month later, I go back to the Hangar. I am barely through the door when the owner calls me.

'Ah, there you are. Where have you been?'

'We've been away touring. Why?'

'There's a guy looking for you. He's been calling every day. You've made another conquest. He left his phone number.'

It's Carlos of course. I check in the phone book: it's a Canadian number.

'Finally! I've called all the gay clubs and bars in Rome. I thought you had disappeared.'

'Why are you looking for me?'

It's obvious of course.

'Because I am in love with you.'

My breath catches in my throat. I haven't stopped thinking about him either.

'I want to see you again,' he says, quickly. 'Can I come over?'

'Of course, but Canada and Italy are not exactly neighbours.'

Three days later he lands in Rome. He will be here for one week, our 'honeymoon' – a very different honeymoon from the one I spent with Clay, an uneducated country boy. Carlos is cultured, sophisticated and romantic. It's impossible to imagine a more desirable man.

A gorgeous bouquet of flowers awaits me at every one of my performances, which drives the other dancers crazy with jealousy, and Carlos always stops over in Rome when he flies to Europe for a conference. I tell him I love the colour purple, and a few days later a huge bouquet of white roses is delivered to me, along with a little can of lavender paint and a card from Carlos, which reads: 'I have travelled the world looking for purple roses, without success. If you like purple so much, paint these white roses in your favourite colour!'

Carlos's cards are always full of imagination and humour. My birthday is 13 August, but Carlos's card arrives on the first, hand illustrated with letters and brightly coloured drawings, and the next day another card arrives, then another, and again another, and so on, a different card for each day, until 13 August.

'Why thirteen cards?'

'Spread them out side by side from the first to the last and you'll see.'

The message I decipher makes me smile with happiness: 'I will always love you'.

Carlos loves the anecdote about the New York bar where whites who like Asians say they are looking for rice and Asians who like whites say that they're into potatoes. He calls me 'rice' and I call him 'potato' and he sends me a recipe for rice potatoes: 'Ingredients: mix Chinese rice and Italian potatoes. Pick a mellow bed and clean, silky sheets. Add soft music and dim the lights.'

Michel Vanuck, a former member of Maurice Béjart's ballet company, offers to take me to Belgium with his company, and I accept immediately. I am happy in Rome – I have a comfortable life, make a decent living, adore Italian men and love the style – but my creativity is withering. I am still choreographing commercials for TV, but I don't dance enough, and certainly not enough modern dance. Brussels on the other hand is alive with the avant-garde. Belgium is not as beautiful as Italy, but it is a less conservative country, less conformist, perhaps because, historically, bilingual countries are more tolerant.

In Brussels, I begin to feel that I can get back into modern dance. At the end of the tour, I listen to my instincts and decide to stay; I give the keys to my Rome apartment to a friend who is returning there, and ask him to send on my clothes.

'What's up with you all of a sudden? What are you going to live on? And what about your furniture?'

'You can sell it, or keep it for yourself if you like. I'll find a way to make a living.'

While I was in Rome I had made the decision to have surgery, and now in Brussels I can get back into choreography. For me it is essential that dance comes first, both as an expression of creativity and as a way of making a living. Becoming a woman is all very well, but then what? Without dance, how do I make a living?

I take classes at the Royal Conservatory of Brussels every day and when the modern dance instructor is unwell I am asked to replace him. At the end of the first class, the students ask the administrator to hire me as their teacher. I have a job again, just like that.

One night I dream that Carlos flies in from Canada with thirteen cans of Coca-Cola in his luggage. But we are not in China and it's easy to find Coke in Belgium. Why did he bring so much with him? I tell Carlos my dream and he laughs. Those are the Coca-Cola cans from my Paris trip coming back to haunt me, as though I were still the little Chinese boy thirsty for the West.

Two months later Carlos comes to Brussels for a conference and at the airport he hands me a box filled with thirteen cans of Coke. His romantic gestures never fail to bowl me over, but I have to remember that he is married. I do not want to be the third wheel – our love deserves more. There is a Chinese saying that it is better to destroy ten temples than to break up a marriage, and Carlos cannot stand cheating on his wife either. He tells her everything.

He doesn't know I have decided to change sex and this decision weighs heavily upon our relationship. He loves me as a man. Why would he stay with me if I became a woman? One day, I decide to call his wife. I want to be straight with her.

'We love the same man, you and I, but he has to make the decision. It is not your fault, nor is it mine. You've loved him for fifteen years, and I've just fallen in love with him. We love each other, but I don't know if we can live together. I don't know if I am the right person for him.'

She doesn't seem surprised by my call. Her voice is calm and warm.

'Carlos has talked to me about you. He says you are a very attractive boy, very nice.'

'I don't want to break up your family. It's the last thing I want.'

Either she is extraordinarily cool, or she's known for a long time that her husband is gay. She continues in a quiet voice.

'I hope we meet one day. In the meantime, let's see what happens.'

Next time I see Carlos I buy a present for Susan and ask him to pass on my greetings.

I also teach at the Dance Academy in Bruges, and Carlos comes to see me there the next time he is in Belgium. He takes photos of me with the students and then we go for lunch beside the canal. It is grey and misty outside, a typical autumn day in northern Belgium. A thin drizzle slides down the restaurant windows and patters on the surface of the canal. Carlos puts his hand on mine. His eyes are tender, determined.

'Come and live with me in Canada.'

So the moment has come. I have prepared for it. I can only stay with him if he accepts my decision. But how can he accept it?

'No, I can't.'

'Why?'

'Because I am going to go back to China to have an operation to become a woman.'

His beautiful, expressive face darkens.

'Why do you need to do that?'

'Because that's what I feel. You are homosexual, but deep down I feel like a woman.'

He pulls back, looking offended. My words have hurt him.

'Not homosexual: bisexual. That's not the same thing. I have been married for fifteen years, don't forget that.'

I shake my head. I am going to give him a fatal blow, but I must be honest with him. He has to face himself, otherwise his life will continue to be a lie and his marriage a fake.

'You are gay, Carlos. You don't realize it, but I know it's true. You have a very good relationship with Susan, but you love me because I am a man. It's a man you are looking for, a man with whom you want to make a life. It's the man in me that you love. Not the woman I will become. It can't work between us.'

Men are so handsome when they cry. They don't cry with big, noisy sobs, but with silent tears. Carlos has defended himself so often: no, he isn't gay, he just needs both a wife and a lover-boy. He is bi, that's all. Such things happen. But this time he doesn't protest.

He lets the tears run down his face without wiping them off. For so many years he has told himself those lies; it has taken this long to accept himself. And now it is over between us. His face loosens behind the tears. His beautiful hands open out on the table between us.

'Yes,' he says, 'maybe you're right.'

'I love you. But life is splitting us apart, sending us in different directions.'

When I think of our break-up, it's this image that stays with me: the image of a middle-aged man sitting across from me, his handsome face dissolving into tears, while outside the rain falls onto a canal as it flows through the little, old-fashioned town. And I remember Carlos's words when we say goodbye for the last time: 'You will always have the key to my heart.'

⌒

Two men walk into the sauna of a gay bathhouse in Brussels. The one I notice is only 1.7 metres at most, not like the tall, well-built men I am usually attracted to, but he has beautiful eyes. Our eyes meet briefly and I feel the impact of his gaze: self-confident, powerful and luminous. He has the look of a man who knows exactly what he wants. He lies down on the wooden bench next to his companion without saying anything, and leaves after a few minutes. Later, while I am drying off, he comes up to me. Without even asking for my name he slips his card into my hand and says, 'Call me.' It reads: 'Mr E, Esquire'.

I call him a few days later. He is married and the father of twins. Sexually, hardly anything happens between us. He takes me in his arms and caresses me, that's all. One night, I invite him to a gala at the Royal Conservatory. The performance is followed by a cocktail party attended by the royal family and high-ranking government officials. During the evening, Philippe, the son of the director of the Conservatory, takes me aside.

'If you need a Belgian passport, I can introduce you to the top lawyer in the country. This man wins all his cases; you can have complete faith in him. Plus he's a Member of Parliament.'

He shows me the man he is talking about, who is chatting with other guests at the bar. It is Mr E. He talks to everyone, including the director of the Conservatory, and they all seem to show him a lot of respect. I observe him from a distance, since I am not supposed to know him, and wait for Philippe to introduce us officially. Mr E, playing the same game, congratulates me on my performance. At the end of the evening, he takes me home in his car, and I shake his hand.

'Delighted to hear you are a famous big-shot lawyer.'

He turns on the ignition and shrugs.

'So what?'

I find out he is the lawyer for an Italian mafia clan and that he has defended them in several trials. He owns a house in Sicily. He takes me to dinner at the best Italian restaurants in Brussels, he knows all the owners. They always set up a table for us behind a screen to give us some privacy, and invariably they remember our favourite wines and dishes. If I happen to arrive early for one of our dates, they give me the same welcome and attention. When I am too busy with rehearsals to go food shopping, Mr E stops by at my place and fills my refrigerator.

Every day in Brussels on my way to the Royal Conservatory, I walk through the tiny Chinese neighbourhood near La Monnaie, the Royal Opera House. I feel the Chinese lettering taunts me, especially the two ideograms that form the word 'China'. They follow me, call out to me. I walk faster. I don't want to hear what they are telling me. My life is sweet and quiet in Brussels. I live in a pretty building in the old town and I have two lovers: Mr E, and a Dutch boyfriend who comes to see me on weekends. A young British baker whose shop is opposite my building brings me fresh bread in the morning and on Saturdays and Sundays I help out at the till. I teach. I dance. I have no desire to go back to China. And yet I can't ignore the ideograms, whose calls get louder and louder. Sometimes I buy ingredients for Manchurian dishes from a Chinese grocery store, and on Sundays I go to the big antiques fair and stroll down the alleys lined with *chinoiseries*. I admire the stalls with their array of porcelain and lacquered boxes, bolts of gold-embroidered silk. When I lived in China I dreamt of the West, and now that I am here, now that the novelty has subsided, I see China through different eyes. Those artefacts are testament to one of the oldest and most refined civilizations in the world. I pick up a red lacquered bowl and trace its smooth curve with my finger. The lacquer shines like the surface of a lake. I unfold scrolls of rice-paper parchment whose rigorous and voluptuous calligraphy soars like ballet jetés. The blue of the china is as clear as a child's eyes. My chest swells with pride. I am ashamed of those Chinese who live abroad and have only contempt for their ancestral culture. If a foreigner happens to die in China, officials either make amends or offer their condolences, but if a Chinese man dies far from his native land, the foreigners couldn't care less.

When I was in the army, I thought patriotism was pure propaganda. But now, each time I pace the streets of Chinatown, my heart tightens a little further. After Chinese New Year 1993, I seriously begin to dread the ideograms. I can see they are trying to attract me, seduce me, but they trouble my mind. I change my route to the Conservatory, hoping that by keeping my distance from the Chinese streets, my desire to return home will vanish.

Throughout the winter I think about the operation. I haven't met any other transsexuals since Rome. I know that the transsexual community is minuscule, but I will have to find it sooner or later. I consult with a famous Belgian surgeon, a world specialist in sex reassignment surgery. From behind his desk he shares his knowledge with me, talks about his success rate. He describes the operation: the opening of the penis, what happens to the foreskin, the nerve endings and the head, all the technical details. He tells me about the compulsory two years of psychiatric treatment, and about the pre-op year I must spend dressed as a woman to test my psychological ability to handle the switch. Throughout our appointment, he barely looks at me. His hands fly over the medical illustrations. I picture myself laid out on the operating table like a piece of meat between his competent hands, his gloved fingers picking up one surgical tool after another.

'Are you ready? When would you like to begin the process?'

He still doesn't look at me, just leafs through his appointments book. He is a professional, this doctor. You can tell that his handiwork will be precise and flawless, without a single false move or blunder. But I will be putting my life in his hands. In my heart, I am very scared. I am uncertain. I have so many questions to ask him: what he thinks of my body, if I am a good candidate, what are the risks, if it's really possible to become a bona fide woman, if society eventually accepts you as such. I would like to tell him that I don't need the two years of therapy, that I have been ready for ten years at least, and that in any case I can't afford it. Also that I would never walk around dressed as a woman as long as I am physically a man; in my culture, that's just not right. But I feel comfortable with him. I don't say anything.

He is waiting for my answer, pen in hand. He looks up at me and, right in that moment I know that it is unthinkable: I could never entrust my life to this man. We have nothing in common. I grip the arms of my chair.

'Thank you. I need to think it through some more.'

He shakes my hand.

'Well, call me when you have made your decision.'

I walk back through the centre, through the little streets of Chinatown. This time, the Chinese characters soothe me. I don't resist them. I was born in China, it is in China that I must be reborn as a woman: I must go home.

My mother's phone call surprises me because she gets straight to the point, dispensing with niceties and adopting an imperious tone.

'Jin Xing, you've been gone a long time. You must come back to China.'

'My God! I was thinking the same thing, but I am not ready.'

'The time has come,' she says, ignoring my excuse.

'You are right. I feel it is God's will.'

The real reason I want to return is for the operation, but of course my mother knows nothing about that. It is my secret. China's medical equipment and hospital system are not as good as the West's, but my native land will protect me, I am convinced of it.

The very next day I resign from the Royal Conservatory. I pack, give my furniture to my friends, just as I did when I left Rome, and before that when I left Beijing. I am ready to leave within a fortnight.

At eleven o'clock the night before I am due to fly home, the phone rings just as I am about to fall asleep. It's Mr E.

'I am downstairs. Can I come up?'

'I was asleep. I am flying back to China tomorrow.'

'What? Why didn't you call me to say goodbye? Is there an emergency?'

'No, but I feel I must go back. I've just decided.'

'Come down. I want to speak to you.'

'It's too late. My plane leaves early in the morning.'

'Not even to drink a last beer with me?'

His voice is pressing.

'OK,' I relent. 'I'm coming down.'

In the car we kiss without saying a word. He drives round and round the streets of Brussels, fast, without stopping at any of our usual bars. We will not drink a last beer together. I know how complex his heart is. I glance at him. He is crying. He pulls up in a dark side street.

I put my hand on his.

'My life is about to change. I have to leave.'

'Good luck, Jin Xing. If you need anything, don't hesitate to come and see me.'

2

Back in Beijing I barely recognize my mother, her hair has turned so white in the last five years. The airport also saddens me. Compared to the ultra-modern airports I have been used to, full of glass and mirrors and expensive boutiques, Beijing airport looks old and dirty. Nevertheless, when I arrive at the huge house in which my mother has been living since her divorce, I sleep like I haven't slept since I left China. The sky could have fallen in, a typhoon could have hurtled past the window, and still I would not have been roused from my deep and peaceful slumber. Could it be that in all my years abroad I never really slept properly? I see now why Chinese emigrants are so keen to come back home for their final years. Abroad, we're in someone else's home, and though we appreciate the life they offer us, there is no real bond. It is hard to relax fully.

'Mum, don't you think it's weird that I have never had a girlfriend?'

I take her by surprise, but I need to deal with this. She lifts her eyes from the book she is reading.

'You have always been so devoted to your career. That's a good thing. You'll have plenty of time for a girlfriend later, after you've turned thirty.'

Can she really believe what she is saying? Or is she hedging?

'Mum, please stop fooling yourself. Look at me.'

I take my long hair in my hands and fan it out over my shoulders.

'Don't you think I look like a woman?'

She puts down her book – her face doesn't betray a thing – folds her hands in her lap and speaks in a quiet voice.

'Yes, especially now, with your hair long. We've always said that, actually, since you were a little boy. You are a lot more sensitive and delicate than your sister.'

'Mum, it's because I am a woman. That's why. I was destined to be female.'

A shadow passes over her face.

'What are you talking about, female? You are a man.'

'My body is a man's body, but in my head, in my soul, I am a woman. And I am going to become a woman.'

A frown cleaves her forehead and her hands clench between her knees. Surprise ripples across her features, or perhaps total incomprehension.

'What are you talking about? Why? You are fine as you are.'

I get up so that she can see me clearly and hear me, once and for all; so that she stops pretending.

'I am not fine. Not at all.'

She lowers her head.

'You are fine like this. You can live like this all your life.'

'Don't be selfish!'

'You can be gay. That's not a problem. You wouldn't be the first one.'

'Mum, I am not gay. I want to have a sex-change operation.'

Her hands are pressed even tighter between her knees.

'But how?'

'It's an operation that has been practised in the West for years.'

'But it must be dangerous. And what if it doesn't work? You'll be risking your life, and what about your career? Could you still dance?'

'Yes, of course.'

I tell her about the Italian TV presenter. I tell her that in my career being a woman would be an asset, that it will open doors for me. And, most importantly, I would be at peace with myself. I speak with a firm, steady voice to reassure her.

'For me it doesn't matter whether you are a man or a woman. You will always be my child. But why would you do something so crazy? I don't want you to hurt yourself, do you understand? That's what scares me. Please… stay the way you are.'

Three days after my return to China, I am woken by a phone call from someone in the Ministry of Culture's Arts Department.

'How would you like to teach choreography at national level? There will be two workshops, one in the north and one in the south.'

I am speechless. I only just came back from the West and already I am being offered a very exciting position. The prospect fills me with passion and energy. I ask where exactly they are to take place.

'In Daqing in Manchuria's oil-producing region, and in Fuzhou.'

Even better. The names of both cities are good omens. Daqing means 'the Great Celebration' and Fuzhou 'Fortunate Ocean'.

That evening, her elbows planted on the table and her head turned to one side, my mother can barely hide her tears.

'No sooner are you back than you are leaving again! My house isn't a hotel! We are going to be separated again for another five or six years.'

It's not easy living with my mother after all those years of freedom abroad. After such a long absence she doesn't want to let me go. She wants to know everything, where I am going, what I am doing, as though I were a little boy. I don't have a mobile phone yet, only a pager. One night, while I'm at a meeting with my dancers I get this message: 'Your mother has had a traffic accident, come back immediately.' My God! My mother's had an accident! I drop everything, jump into a cab and rush home. I find my mother sitting in front of the TV, comfortably ensconced in her armchair.

'Mum! What's with the message that you had a traffic accident?'

She doesn't even bother to take her eyes off the TV.

'I fell off my bike and scratched my leg.'

She lifts up her skirt to show me her knee adorned with a tiny plaster.

'But I thought it was a serious accident!'

'Not at all. But it was time for you to come back.'

'Are you kidding? I am twenty-six!'

'Do you know what time it is? Past ten o'clock. If you must have a meeting, schedule it at nine in the morning, not ten at night. At this time of night you should be at home with your mother.'

'Do you realize how much you scared me?'

She carries on watching TV, confident that she's well within her rights. I am seething. She may be my mother, gentle and loving, but she can also be an unbearable tyrant. She loves me, but she is lonely, and so she unloads her frustration and anger onto me.

My length of service in the army entitles me to the rank of colonel and a teaching position, so I fly back to Shenyang to resume my place in the dance troupe; but they are not interested. As far as they are concerned, I left the army without authorization so they don't owe me anything. I will have to manage on my own.

After teaching another choreography class, I create a modern dance show with my students, financed by the Beijing Arts Institute (my alma mater), the Chinese Dancers' Association and my mother. It is China's first privately funded show, and the first major performance of modern dance in the People's Republic. I call it *Half-Dream*, after the dance I created for the American Dance Festival in North Carolina.

Beijing's Baoli Theatre agrees to rent us the theatre half-price, and the Institute lends us a vacant, unheated studio. A freezing draught pierces through the broken windows but we rehearse without a break. The night before the premiere I help the stagehands install the set and the lighting and when the dancers arrive in the morning I start the rehearsal. Adrenaline keeps me up all day and after a coffee and a shower I dance eight pieces out of the ten that comprise the show. One of the pieces is a duet entitled 'Islet', which I dance half-naked with another male dancer. Nobody has ever danced half-naked in the People's Republic before. My friends, who are sitting in the first row, keep glancing over their shoulders for fear the police will turn up and stop the performance. In truth, we are wearing flesh-coloured leotards. And in any case, the police don't show up.

The show is sold out. All the luminaries from Beijing's art and culture circles are there. The curtain calls last at least ten minutes – extremely rare in China, where spectators are in the habit of rushing for the exits as soon as the curtain falls.

The success of *Half-Dream* gives Shenyang's armed services pause for thought; as I am such a talented artist, they really should keep hold of me. They offer me civilian status and a four-room apartment. But it is too late – I, too, have changed my mind. I do not want to go back into the army fold. Military culture abhors the kind of individualism that fuels modern dance. And, anyway, how will I keep my position when I become a woman? So here I am, free at last – and free also to start looking for a hospital for my operation. That, after all, is why I came back home.

The night after the performance of *Half-Dream* I meet Cheng Fangyuan, a pop and folk singer who's very famous in China and who also happens to be the wife of one of my classmates from Shenyang. She sings accompanied by an acoustic guitar and has a very contemporary style, even though she's never been to the West. She asks me to collaborate with her on her new show, *Blue Feelings*. It is such a great offer, and will open so many doors for me in the music world, that the operation will just have to wait.

⌒

Dr Yang Peiying makes me think of Guanyin, the Buddhist Goddess of Mercy, with her serene face and clear complexion. She doesn't express any surprise when I explain the purpose of my visit, as though changing sex was the most ordinary thing in the world. In her office she asks me what I am hoping for. She has never performed sex reassignment surgery, her only experience is with hermaphrodites, and yet I trust her immediately and entirely. I share my worries with her: my beard is very thick, my legs hairy. It is an ironic twist of fate that I have a lot of male hormones. But that doesn't bother her.

'Your chances are good. We can start the first operation whenever you are ready.'

After that meeting, I have to travel back to the States, to Las Vegas, to organize a big acrobatics show sponsored by the Hong Kong Chamber of Commerce. While I am there, I buy myself some dresses, shoes and lingerie. I try everything on to make sure it will fit me. But with the tops, I hesitate. How big will my breasts be? I decide to go for the sexiest, silkiest and most suggestive ones, regardless. The Hong Kong businessman who is accompanying me is surprised to see me arrive back at the hotel weighed down with shopping bags from the most elegant boutiques the city has to offer.

'It's for my girlfriend.'

'Your girlfriend will be in seventh heaven, you're really spoiling her! It's a whole wardrobe you've got there.'

'To tell you the truth I have two girlfriends, and both wear the same size. Convenient, don't you think?'

The Hong Kong businessman laughs and throws me a knowing look.

⁓

'His blood will flow the year he turns twenty-eight.'

I remember the Manchurian astrologer's prediction when Dr Yang calls to let me know there'll be a room available right after Chinese New Year. By the Western calendar, I will turn twenty-eight in August, but according to Chinese tradition, age is determined from conception, not the day of birth. There were no rooms available until this point, and now the hospital doors have suddenly opened. So the year has come when my blood will flow. It's up to me to fulfil the prediction.

'I have a date set for the first operation. It will be 8 February.'

My mother is preparing dim sum – a fiddly culinary activity which demands all her attention.

'What for?'

She is slipping the pale dough into the simmering oil and pushing it around with the tip of the spatula.

'Mum, don't you remember when we talked about my sex-change operation?'

A drop of boiling oil splashes onto her hand and she holds it under the cold tap.

'What operation?'

'Mum! You know very well what I am talking about!'

'No!'

'Yes.'

'You are crazy!'

'It's vital for me.'

She shrugs with barely repressed anger and answers in a grouchy voice, smacking the plate of dim sum on the table. Neither of us touch them.

'You do what you want. But don't count on me to pay for it.'

'I am not asking you for anything. I will pay for everything myself.'

'It's a big risk. Think again. I don't want you to damage yourself.'

She insists on meeting Dr Yang. She wants her to explain everything – the major points at least. Mostly she wants to know what the risks are. She is scared the operation will destroy me. She doesn't approve but, as she has done many times before, she eventually accepts my decision.

Cheng Fangyuan, the pop singer, doesn't approve either. Her eyes grow wide with astonishment and concern when I go to her place to tell her the news.

'An operation? What kind of operation? Is there something wrong?'

'It's a major operation. I am going to become a woman.'

'What? Are you out of your mind? What are you going to be like?'

'I don't know.'

'You are sick, Jin Xing. You are very attractive the way you are. You are a man with something feminine about you. You are very ambiguous, sexually, and that's your charm.'

'Maybe it's fine for you lot. You have a special friend, with ambiguous sexuality. What about me? It doesn't work for me to be ambiguous. I want to be clear with myself. Don't you think it's weird that we are so close, you and I, so comfortable when we are together?'

She stares at me.

'Yes, it's true. We get on very well.'

'We are like two women together. I bet you even forget sometimes that I am a man.'

Her husband, who has been listening to the conversation for a while without saying anything, tries to convince me.

'Jin Xing, you don't even realize how attractive you are. Even to me, and I am not gay. It's your appearance, but also your way of being. You have a lot of charm. Don't change anything.'

They are getting on my nerves, these two. I am not going to give up on the operation just to please them.

'You're being selfish. OK, fine, everybody finds me attractive. But what about me, then? I want to feel good about myself.'

'Wait a bit longer,' Cheng Fangyuan says. 'Do it later, maybe. But look: women are fascinated by you, and men are intrigued. If you become a woman, women won't want to be friends with you and guys won't be turned on by you any more. And as far as men, real men, go... Do you think they're going to want you? They want a natural woman, not... not...'

'A fake one? Is that what you want to say?'

Cheng Fangyuan looks away, embarrassed.

'I don't care. I need to be true to myself, I need to feel at peace. I am ready to lose everything.'

They say nothing.

SHANGHAI TANGO

1

A mauve glow seeps into the rectangle of the open door and bathes the metal bedstead. Red lights flash across an electronic display unit and their pulse seems to accelerate into a kind of vibrating staccato which takes my breath away. My leg! A throbbing pain grips my left leg, as if thousands of little needles are piercing the skin from my knee down to my foot and a thousand-volt current is blasting through my nerves. I try to sit up but my wrists and ankles are attached to various tubes.

A shadow slips by my bed. It's Wang Di, who must have slept in the adjacent room. He hands me a glass of water.

'You must be tired?'

'My leg – something's wrong. Pull the blanket off me, please.'

'Go back to sleep. It's nothing.'

'No, show me.'

He lifts the sheet.

'Turn on the light. Oh my God! What's that?'

My left leg is so swollen that the ankle is bigger than my thigh. I can barely see the tips of my toes, which are buried in the puffed-up flesh. I have no sensation between my knee and my toes.

'My God! I am screwed. I'm going to jump out the window!'

'Don't freak. It'll get better.'

I fall into a drugged drowsiness. The next day the swelling has still not subsided. The skin is so stretched it glistens with a purple sheen. A pin prick and the whole leg might explode. I don't even think about the sixteen-hour operation that has just taken place. Everything's fine on that front, the nurse tells me. Total success. They've installed a catheter and stuffed me with gauze like a baby. There was only one hitch – a haemorrhage that the doctors weren't able to stop for four hours, which has caused a dramatic weight loss – but everything's back in order now. A haemorrhage! But of course, that's the bloody episode predicted by the astrologer. In spite of the complications, for some reason I am hopeful. Things are progressing according to the Heavens. I am a woman. But the pain is unbearable.

Dr Yang arrives with a nurse. Her tired features light up when she sees me.

'Look at her,' she says to the nurse. 'Her face has changed. She looks like a woman already. Don't you think? Congratulations!'

No need to congratulate me. I feel like neither woman nor man; I feel only excruciating pain.

'What about my leg?'

'Your leg slipped off the stirrup and we didn't realize it right away. Your calf was pressing against the iron stirrup for a while, which interrupted the flow of blood to the muscle.'

'The nerves must have been damaged. I have no sensation in my leg.'

'We'll know more tomorrow when the neurologists come. Jin Xing...'

She takes my hand. Her touch reassures me a little.

'We'll do everything in our power to put you back on your feet.'

She is pale, perhaps from fatigue. An intense, sixteen-hour operation, most of it spent on her knees, must be exhausting. She looks lost.

It is impossible to sleep. The pain grips my leg with red-hot pokers. In the middle of the night, I beg the nurse to give me a shot of morphine.

My mother didn't want to watch the operation, but as soon as I call her the next day she rushes over to the hospital. She is talking to the neurologist, the sports doctor and Dr Yang in the next room and I can hear her crying but not what she is saying. It must be very serious. The door opens and one of the doctors walks out, followed by my mother. He leaves us alone. I give her a questioning look. She is livid.

'So, happy with yourself? Look what you've done! The doctors told me that you can say goodbye to your career. You'll be lucky if you can walk...' She is sobbing so hard she can barely finish.

I don't want to listen to her furious, anguished voice or hear those halting words. I let myself sink back into the cottony vapours of the anaesthetics and opiates.

'Please, don't cry.'

I can hear her voice in the corridor again. She won't let up.

'If Jin Xing can't dance any more she has no reason to live. Dancing is her life. If she had been a mediocre dancer, OK, fine. But she dances so well.'

Is it my mother who's making that speech? My mother who didn't want me to enrol in the army? I could scream with frustration. And Dr Yang's voice, barely recognizable, 'What have I done, my God? What have I done? I have destroyed the career of a talented dancer!'

If I had a knife I would stick it in the bloated skin of my leg to burst it open. I would slash my leg at the knee in order to sleep. Just to sleep. But the rare minutes of drowsiness are interrupted by throbbing blows of pain. At the end of the day Dr Yang brings me the test results and the diagnosis. The nerves are dead from the calf down to the toes. That explains the lack of sensation in my leg. In cases like this, it is difficult to regain the use of the leg. There are possible treatments, but at best I will limp till the end of my days.

Dr Yang looks like she has aged ten years. Her skin is a dull yellow and her cheeks are hollow. She puts a box full of sweets on my bedside table. I look at her without really hearing her. This must be a morphine-induced nightmare, I think to myself. I will wake up soon.

'It's not your fault,' I manage to mumble. 'It's the nurses' fault, for sure. During the second operation, do you remember, they were chatting in a corner and gave you the wrong scalpel.'

Dr Yang makes a small, imperceptible gesture with her hand and speaks in a voice overcome with weariness.

'Jin Xing, I am responsible. We will do everything we can, I promise you. We will try everything, acupuncture, massages, rehabilitation. Let's hope for the best.'

We don't even talk about the genital operation: there's nothing to discuss. A nurse changes the dressing stuffed into my vaginal cavity and pulls out bloody cotton balls. It feels as if she is tearing my flesh apart, but I stop myself from hollering. During the few minutes it takes to clean the wound and change the dressing, the pain is so fierce that I even forget my leg.

'In a few weeks, we'll remove the catheter and you'll be able to change the dressing by yourself.'

In the meantime I take only liquid food. To ease the healing process I must not have any bowel movements. The stabbing pain in my leg picks up again, like a fire alarm, after the vaginal care is finished.

The skin on my leg glows purple. Even the touch of the sheet is unbearable. Sacrifice: the word comes to my mind like a bitter balm. It is such a transgression, this transformation from man to woman; why should I not expect to pay a price. Not for me the casualness of the Brazilian transsexuals who have operations on a whim, as though they were going for a simple facelift. For me it is a rebirth. I think of the way a woman's body is torn apart during labour, but it is my self – my true nature – that I am bringing forth into the world. My friends admire my courage, but it takes a lot more than that. Everything has to fall into place at the right time. And indeed, the three operations have been successful. I ask myself if I have made a mistake, whether I am going to have to sacrifice my career to become a woman. I can't really believe that. It is more likely that the path to happiness is a thorny one and God is testing me to see whether I am up to the challenge I have set myself. It is just a hardship I must overcome. Only then will the change be complete. No point complaining: I have chosen my path and I must go to the end of the pain.

These thoughts pound through my head as insistently as the pains shoot up my leg. They haunt me like a litany. When night falls, when the lights are turned off and the rectangle from the open door suffuses the room with its mauve glow, I beg the nurse to give me another shot.

'If we go on like this, it will become a habit. It's the last time.'

'Just to sleep.'

Relief sweeps through me.

The stage at the Beijing Opera House is bathed in light. I am dressed in red and my head is shaved like a monk's. My dancers float towards me and surround me in a half-circle. We dance in silence. And then a voice soars, crystalline, as though this was an opera rather than a modern dance performance, and suddenly the face of the singer appears in front of me. It's Wang Yanyuan and she isn't singing at all. She is watching me without a word.

'Wang Yanyuan! What are you doing here? Aren't you supposed to be in New York?'

She touches my cheek. Her skin is cool.

'I am in Beijing for a performance. I heard my little brother had become my little sister. So I came to the hospital.'

She bursts into tears.

I slowly come out of my opiate sleep.

'My God, why did you destroy yourself like that?'

Tears run down her face.

'Come on, Wang Yanyuan, don't cry. I am so happy to see you.'

'What happened? Your leg is damaged, I heard? And you are so skinny!'

I tell her about the four-hour haemorrhage, about the fifteen kilograms I lost, and about my leg, how it slipped off the stirrup and the calf got crushed. I lift the sheet to show her. Her face turns white with horror. She runs over to the nurses.

'Incompetents! Don't you realize what you've done! You've destroyed Jin Xing's career. Do you hear me?' She screams so loud her voice breaks. 'If she had been a lousy dancer, she could consider doing something else with her life, but she is a major talent!'

'Wang Yanyuan, stop it! Calm down. We'll find a solution.'

'What solution? There's only one solution: sue the hospital.'

'No way!'

'Yes. You are handicapped for life. You must be compensated. How are you going to survive? If you win the case, at least you'll have enough to live on.'

It's obvious Wang Yanyuan has been living in New York for a long time. It's the all-purpose American response: sue the doctors and fill your pockets.

'But you know the system here. If I sue Dr Yang, she will lose everything. It's the nurses who should be punished.'

'What do you care about the system? It's your life that's in the balance.'

'Please stop screaming. Calm down.'

But she doesn't give up on the idea. She finds a Chinese lawyer in New York who flies to Shanghai to see me and discuss the case. We'll claim ten million *yuan* in compensation – and that's letting them off lightly, they both agree. The sum blows my mind. Ten million *yuan*! That's almost a million US dollars, but at China's standard of living it is really ten or even a hundred times more. Who in China could come up with that amount of money? They might as well sell the whole hospital. Dr Yang's reputation would be destroyed. The situation seems intractable. What to do? The question torments me as I lie in bed.

Dr Yang comes to see me and brings me sweets, dishes that she prepares herself. She looks devastated and is getting skinnier by the day. After her examination, she sits down beside my bed.

'I only wanted to help you. And I've destroyed your career.'

I try to console her. But my leg is still very swollen and the acupuncture sessions and the massages don't help very much.

The shot of morphine the nurse gives me every evening is helping me less and less. It must be a sign that I am getting used to it. I train myself to fall asleep in spite of the pain. In the morning, when the nurse lifts the sheet to dress my wounds, I check to see if my toenails are more visible than the day before, or if there's been a change of colour. Sometimes I convince myself that things have improved a little, that the thousand needles pierce me with less intensity, that the flesh around the toes is a tad less puffy, and that the purple has faded overnight. The nurse and I even forget to talk about my vaginal wounds, we are so focussed on what's happening with my leg.

Death could hardly be worse than these never-ending ordeals. They are my Stations of the Cross. I try to understand the lessons they are teaching me. When we have burnt the candle at both ends, the hospital helps us rest. If we've been too proud, the hospital reminds us that glory is worthless. However powerful or famous we might be, in hospital we learn that we cannot control our lives, and that we are all equals. I mull over these philosophical truths in an attempt to come to terms with my situation.

Finally, Wang Yanyuan convinces me that I have to be realistic. There's no other recourse than to sue the hospital. The lawyer flies back from New York with a bulging file under his arm. With a heavy heart I fill out the forms and sign each one. Starting legal proceedings means abandoning any hope of recovery.

I watch from my bed as pale buds appear on the trees and then blossom into luminous halos. I checked into hospital at the beginning of February, in midwinter; now spring is arriving. The Hospital of the Perfumed Hills is located in a famously beautiful area, popular with high-ranking military officers on vacation. Autumn, they say, is especially spectacular, but I hope I won't stay long enough to see the leaves turn red. The renewal of nature brings tenuous hope and yet, even though the swelling is slowly going down, there is still no sensation in my leg. I push away the sheet and, as I do every day, try with all my might to send an impulse to my leg, as though with sheer will-power I might be able to force the nerves and muscles back to life. I stare at my left foot for a long time, mentally ordering it to move.

My God! My toes are quivering. I lean forward as much as I can and, once again, yes! I catch the slightest of movements. A wave of insane joy engulfs me. I call for a nurse and she, too, observes my left foot. With a huge effort of concentration I manage to move my toes ever so slightly. The nurse confirms it: I am not hallucinating. If my toes are moving, that means the nerves are beginning to function again. So there is hope. Dr Yang, summoned right away, verifies the barely perceptible tremble of my toes. We are ecstatic. My heart fills with wild hope and I call the lawyer to tell him to abandon the legal proceedings. Then I ask the doctors to arrange a meeting and devise a treatment plan.

An ambulance picks me up every day to drive me to the Sports Medicine Department of Beijing University's Third Hospital, where my rehabilitation is taking place. I have electro-acupuncture to stimulate the nerve endings. The swelling in my leg begins to go down, slowly at first, then faster and faster, and the pain abates enough for me to tell the nurse we can stop the morphine shots. She laughs. I ask her what's so funny – it's really no laughing matter. She leans over me and confides, 'Jin Xing, they weren't shots of morphine.'

I stare at her. What does she mean?

'The first three nights, yes, but we were worried that you would become dependent on the morphine, so since then we've been giving you shots of saline!'

'I don't understand. I went to sleep anyway?'

'Ah, the power of suggestion!'

After two weeks of treatment I can leave my bed, but only to be carried to a wheelchair. After my initial enthusiasm, progress is so slow that I lose heart again. I abhor the wheelchair, this transportation for invalids. And my vagina is still not completely healed. Normally the catheter is removed two weeks after surgery, but because of my leg I have to keep it for two and a half months. At the beginning, when I take only liquid food, it's relatively easy: I simply open the stopcock on the catheter duct to allow urination. But when I start to eat solid food, going to the toilet becomes a nightmarish ordeal: holding the gauze stuffing inside my vagina with one hand, blood dripping down my thighs, I must balance on one leg while the other one is propped up on a bench. It is quite a feat and makes me break into such a sweat that I need a good fifteen minutes to return to bed and another fifteen minutes to catch my breath.

I am totally unprepared for the atrocious pain I feel when the catheter has to be changed. I scream and holler and thrash about, but the nurse is unperturbed and swears things will be fine as soon as the new one is in place. But as soon as she is done a new pain, just as unbearable, begins. Within a few hours my stomach distends. A doctor comes to massage me and after an hour and a half of painful work my urine begins to flow. The next day I have the same problem, the same excruciating pain. A doctor looks into my room to find out what's wrong.

'Could you just have a look? Something's wrong. I think the catheter is pushing against my bladder.'

The doctor is a young intern, unsure of himself. He hesitates. He didn't put the catheter in himself. Perhaps he should get some help.

'Please, can you try? I can't stand it any more. If you pull it just a bit. Yes, like that. A little more. Ahhh!'

All the urine that had again accumulated in the bladder flows out and the pain, miraculously, vanishes.

As soon as I have regained some strength, I refuse the wheelchair and request a pair of crutches. Crutches feel temporary; with them you are on your way to recovery until the day you throw them away and walk firmly on your own two feet, cured. The crutches make me more optimistic. I come back from the rehabilitation centre at the Third Hospital with a little more strength every day, and as soon as I am able, I hop on one crutch, and then I throw away the crutch and limp on a cane.

To compensate me for the accident to my leg, the hospital exempts me from all surgical and accommodation expenses. Dr Yang, however, cannot forgive herself for the negligence that caused the accident. When she brings me sweets I console her and tell her my leg will soon be restored to health, that it's a question of months, perhaps weeks, of perseverance. I tell her that I will recover completely. I point out that I am already so much better than the doctors ever dared hope and that it's a miracle because they had given up on my leg. And I assure her that the nerves are coming back to life and that I will walk again one day, even dance. She must have faith. I wanted to become a woman and that was never going to be simple; there were bound to be complications because it is such a difficult operation.

I am not absolutely convinced myself, but I need to give us both a pep talk, to give us both hope. The nurses cannot believe their ears. They have never heard a patient comforting a doctor – usually the patients heap ill-founded reproaches on the medics, yet in this case the opposite is happening, even though the hospital is so obviously at fault.

Although Dr Yang keeps telling me that I have become inherently more feminine since the surgery, that my features are finer, I feel like neither a woman nor a man, but like a hospital patient. The recovery process takes ages and is terribly painful. The cotton balls wadded into my vagina are meant to help it heal while preventing the opening from sealing back up. Below the clitoris is the hole through which the urine flows, and below that hole, the small vagina. To start with, my vagina is only about ten centimetres deep, but once it's completely healed I have to insert a dilator into it every day to deepen the cavity and make it more flexible, in preparation for sexual intercourse. The first time I introduce the dilator it hurts like all hell! But I have to do it every single day. Doctors recommend frequent sexual intercourse after surgery, in order to improve the vagina's elasticity and depth, but in my case I have to satisfy myself with a medical dildo – not very sexy.

Meanwhile, my libido is at zero, which is hardly surprising considering the pain I'm in, but I think it's because of the hormones. These are routinely prescribed to enhance the body's feminine characteristics, minimize the regrowth of body hair, augment the breasts and make the skin finer. My beard has already been removed and my silicone breasts are in place, so the hormones come next. As soon as I start taking Premarin I notice the difference. By nature I am an optimistic, enthusiastic and energetic person, and yet suddenly I have turned into a moody, lazy woman. Even on good days – after the catheter has been removed and I'm hopping around on a crutch and my sleepy nerves have begun to revive – I lie at the bottom of my bed, devoid of energy or desire, stuffing myself with sweets. I hate that feeling. It's not me. I do have female organs now, but I want to be myself. I have done nothing to change my voice, for instance, which is still manly, not particularly low, but husky. It is possible to operate on the vocal cords and modify the tone of the voice, to turn it from baritone to soprano, for example, but mine is mezzo-soprano and I will keep it like that. I love the contrast between an ultra-feminine appearance and a husky voice – it is surprising, but not really shocking, except in China, where female voices are high-pitched. One day, later, after I have left the hospital, I hail a cab, and when I give the driver the address, he turns around, surprised, his eyebrows knotted.

'It's strange, I could have sworn it was a woman who got into my cab, but you have a man's voice.'

'I was a man before,' I tell him.

'You are kidding!'

'No, it's the truth.'

I take the hormones for six months, on Dr Yang's recommendation, but I don't feel well. If there is even the remotest possibility that

I could dance again, how would I manage with such little energy? I can always slather my skin in emollient creams but I want to be at the top of my form. I stop the hormones. My energy and sexuality come back immediately. I feel alive again.

2

It is a beautiful August day. The trees are covered with thick, luxurious foliage and the blue sky sparkles. I watch the magnificent landscape through the window of the car that takes me back to Beijing, my cane on my lap. The apprehension I felt six months ago on this same road has evolved into a different kind of anxiety. I have managed to withstand the physical pain, but the psychological pain that society will inflict on me concerns me now.

At the hospital the other patients almost forgot that I was a transsexual. They did me little favours, came to chat with me. We were all equal in our suffering, all in the same boat. But to those in the outside world, the healthy ones, the normal ones who have never had to question who they are, my operation and long rehabilitation are the subject of much discussion.

My friends are split into two camps: those who support me completely, and those who are critical. The first group came to visit me and regularly phoned to check how I was. I only know what the others think through the grapevine. They think I got what I deserved; that one doesn't mess with nature with impunity; that I was asking for it; that my career is now over; that I was mad to tempt fate like that; that I must be a sorcerer's apprentice! Their reactions are quite normal, of course, and it would be strange if some people didn't disapprove. Some of them just need time to get used to it. I have not done anything illegal, even according to our stringently communist lawmakers. The only people who I believe are entitled to make demands are my parents, and they support me fully. When my father came back from Shenyang to inform me that he had managed to have my identity changed and that all my documents were officially registered in a woman's name, he said to me, 'Be happy. Live your life.' My father, Mr Conservative! As for my mother, she immediately found neurologists and specialists in sports medicine to discuss potential treatments with the hospital staff, so that I would have nothing but the best treatment.

I let my cane drop to the floor of the car. There will come a day when I will not need it any longer, but the critics' choir will not stop. I swear to myself that I will get back onstage and show them all what I am capable of.

Before checking into hospital, all those months ago, I had moved into a large traditional house with a square courtyard in a famous compound belonging to the Shi family. My eighty-year-old landlady, a former doctor at the Beijing Gynaecology and Obstetrics Hospital, inherited the house on the death of her husband, who was Chairman Mao's dentist. She lives in the building overlooking the front courtyard, and I live at the back.

My mother is waiting for me in the courtyard, her face impassive. She watches me alight awkwardly from the car with my cane, before offering me her arm so that I can lean on her, this old woman giving support to a young one – a *new* one. I take small steps under my long skirt. She has never said a thing to me about the operation, but her close friends have told me that she feels guilty about my leg because she refused to attend the surgery and was not there to take care of me.

She does not yet know how to be around me comfortably. Addressing me is simple – there's no distinction in Chinese between 'he' and 'she' – but when I hear her on the phone to my sister, saying 'your brother' this, 'your brother' that, I yell at her across the room: '"Your sister", Mum, "your sister"!'

My sister lives on Long Island now. She is married to a Korean–American and works for Shiseido, the Japanese cosmetics company. I went to visit her before the operation, on my way back from Las Vegas, but I didn't tell her about the surgery. She is a traditionalist, like our father. It was bad enough when our parents divorced, so imagine her reaction to my news, those howls of indignation!

'But you are absolutely nuts, Jin Xing! Artists are insane. I will never understand. But OK, you'll always be my brother – I mean, my sister.' And she starts to giggle. 'Thank heavens my children are still young; they will grow up with an aunt, not an uncle.'

At breakfast my mother leans towards me and, like a bird of prey skewering its victim, digs two perfect talons into my chin and pulls hard.

'It's ironic, isn't it? You think you can become a woman, and yet you still have hair on your face. Go and pluck them out!'

The removal of the follicles was not a hundred per cent perfect. I will have to finish the job with laser treatments.

Another morning, it's the same little game.

'Oh, you have a little moustache this morning. Go and shave!'

She doesn't ask me anything about my sex life. We never talk about that. But one day she musters all her courage and asks me in an embarrassed voice, 'And, uh… when you pee, uh… everything's normal, yes? Everything's OK? Ah, thank heavens!'

Reassured, she still looks at me with sadness in her eyes.

'You will be alone. No man will want you. It would be good if you had children to keep you company and take care of you when you get old.'

That is not how I think at all. Children are to be loved and cherished, guided onto the right path in life, not kept around to serve as supports for old age. But she is insistent.

'You could adopt.'

I say nothing. What insanity to think about such a distant future when I still can't walk without a cane.

My mother tells all those willing to listen, and some who aren't, that I changed sex for my career. To her my career is sacred – she is so proud of it and it provides her with an 'acceptable' explanation. Most of the time, though, she says nothing, and her silence is comforting to me. She has always taken her time to accept things.

I am still skinny and pale, I have straggly hairs on my face, I dress in long skirts and I wear very little make-up. I need time to make myself beautiful, attractive. I still don't know what kind of woman I want to be. I need to find out.

My first outing is to a party given by a friend who has come back from New York. I am wearing a black miniskirt, my hair hangs loose to my shoulders and I have put on a little make-up. At the door, my friend looks at me without recognizing me.

'Oh my God! It's you!'

She introduces me to everyone.

'I have a very special guest. Guess who she is. Some of you already know her.'

In her bedroom she asks if she can touch my breasts.

'They feel like real ones!'

I tell her she can have the same ones implanted if she wants to.

My friends come and visit me. They observe me warily, unsure at first of how to behave. They look for something ambiguous in my appearance. 'You are still masculine,' they tell me. In their minds, I have been a man and I will always be one. They want to speak to me, touch me freely the way they did in the past, but even my closest friends, those who love me, are hesitant.

In Manchuria, where I am invited to choreograph some military shows, I land wearing a long overcoat and high-heeled boots and with my hair hanging loose down my back. My old friends and teachers look at me sideways. A former classmate asks whether they can all kiss me and I say no, they can't. I am a woman now and things are different. Mr Men holds me tight in his arms and immediately pulls back, uncertain of my reaction. He invites me to sit down.

'You have no idea how much damage you did when you denounced me. I had to retire a year early without getting the promotion I was entitled to.'

My smile freezes on my lips.

'I asked you to let me go, but you refused.'

He sits up and hits the arm of his chair as though to erase old and bitter memories. He watches me for a long while.

'Let's forget all that. I have too much affection for you. You have talent. You are the best choreographer in China.'

'You see,' I say, 'I am not gay. I am a woman. If I hadn't gone to America, I would not be who I am today. You've held a grudge against me, I know that. And I have hated you too. But anger propels us forward in life.'

I hesitate for a moment and then push on. I might as well tell him the truth.

'You know that recording in the hotel room in Beijing, when you made a pass at me? I told you I had given the cassette to the general?'

He waits. Perhaps he already knows what's coming.

'There never was any cassette. I was bluffing.'

The flash of anger in his eyes melts into admiration.

'Bastard!'

The Chinese communist films from the thirties and forties that fascinated me when I was a child were full of heroes fighting the Japanese during the Civil War. But I was always more attracted to the villains, especially as the Japanese generals and Kuomintang officers were always assisted by a well-groomed secretary who would carry their top-secret documents. With a smart uniform cinched at the waist, high heels, handbag and cigarette angled between long, polished nails, she was just the kind of woman I dreamt of becoming: sophisticated, mysterious, glamorous and sexy. A spy, maybe, or a double agent.

When you arrive at the end of a long journey, the destination you have been dreaming of appears like a mirage. You picture an iridescent sea, clear as sapphire, lapping on velvet soft sandy beaches, palaces with crystal chandeliers and elegant avenues along which lovely women click in high-heeled pumps. But even if you have imagined all the details, the reality will still be full of rough edges and awkward angles. I am used to making myself up for the stage, but the business of wearing high heels, tight skirts and handbags requires a dexterity I had not, even with all my dance training, anticipated. I dress up too much and too well. I look like an Italian woman who shops in Las Vegas: hyper-sophisticated and always impeccable, wearing make-up, miniskirts (never trousers, never jeans), pantyhose, long red nails and big rings. In China, that is way too far over the top! And yet somehow I need this staginess and exaggeration to convince myself and the world around me that I am a woman. It is almost like learning a part for a film or the stage. First you have to collect the accessories, visualize the character, play it physically from the outside, and then, little by little, begin to inhabit her from the inside, more fully and honestly.

⌒

The Potala rises, huge and majestic, from the red hill overlooking Lhasa, so close to us that for a brief moment it seems as though the plane is going to land on one of its terraces. It is such a fantastic apparition, this immense temple in the middle of the Himalayas, that I feel purified, and I thank the Heavens for this operation that has made me a woman, even though it left me lame.

'It's an extraordinary landscape, don't you think? Forgive me.'

The man sitting next to me leans across me to get a better glimpse of the palace in its mountain setting.

'Yes, it's a magical sight. It looks like a painting.'

He sits back and smiles at me. He seems shy, but from his formal manners I suspect he is a high-ranking government official. He is travelling with four other men – they were at Chengdu airport when we changed planes – and has asked if he can sit next to me to get a better view as we land. I get the feeling he is interested in me as much as in the Potala, though. With my long green skirt (Las Vegas again), hair pulled into a ponytail, gloves and sunglasses, I must have attracted his attention in Chengdu. It is unusual to see Chinese women wearing gloves, or dressed so elegantly. When I was a man, I used to race through airports so I could be first at check-in, dumping my luggage down any old fashion. Now that I am a woman, I take my time and look after my luggage, because I want my suitcases and bags to be perfect. I enjoy this new role. It is a game. I play the glamorous, sexy starlet. It is a role that suits me.

'You don't look Chinese. You must have lived abroad. Am I right?'

I smile mysteriously. He will find out soon enough who I am.

We go our separate ways at the airport; a delegation from the local government has come to greet him, and a former student of mine from the dance workshop, Ge Zhen, has come to pick me up. She is Tibetan and has invited me to create a solo for her entitled 'Dedication'. I have drawn my inspiration from images and feelings linked to my operation: they symbolize a woman giving birth. I have come to Lhasa for the premiere.

That night, just as I am about to fall asleep in my hotel room, the phone rings. It's the man from the plane. He introduces himself: Mr X, personal secretary to the former premier Zhao Ziyang. He apologizes for calling so late and hopes he is not disturbing me. He met some dancers from my company at a banquet given in his honour and discovered I was staying at the Tibet Hotel and he would love to meet up. He suggests a drink, now, if it's not too late...

I am tired but he intrigues me. And, to be honest, I am impressed. The personal secretary to the former premier! We meet at the hotel bar. His eyes remind me of Mr E, the Belgian lawyer; they are the eyes of a predator. He is a handsome, solid, powerful man; traditional communist mentality; direct. I like that. He is travelling with colleagues from Beijing Central Government.

'We are going on a trip tomorrow to the outskirts of Lhasa for a few days. Would you like to join us?'

It is a great opportunity. Government officials have special access to places that ordinary people can never visit. We drive in a car with his entourage and spend the first night together. The dancers have told him my story and I confess to him that it is the first time I have made love as a woman. I am a little apprehensive, but he is perfect and very gentle. He doesn't want to hurt me and acts like a real gentleman. He touches my cheek with a tender finger, saying, 'You still have a little hair.' I am moved by this gesture. He is married, however, and I already know there is no future for us. To be the mistress of a high-ranking Chinese official might be possible in secret, but we could never be together in public.

The Yangbajing hot springs gush forth dramatically from the heart of the Himalayas. Mr X asks the driver to stop the car and we go down to buy bathing suits from the little shop nearby. One of them is purple and of course I pick that one. He and I are alone in the pool. The air is very cold – we are at a very high altitude, not far off 5000 metres – yet the water is hot. Steam hovers above the surface of the water and we try to hide ourselves in its vapours. I pretend I don't know how to swim so that he can take me in his arms and help me. While he caresses me under the water, his assistants and under-secretaries, stiff with cold in their overcoats and scarves, watch us with stern looks.

We pile back into the car and Mr X soon asks the driver to pull up a second time. Again, the two of us alight and walk a little way along a steep path, while the others stay in the warm car. We lean over a little bridge and watch the torrent rushing below us, channelled between the rock faces. Mr X presses himself against me and I am filled with a profound melancholy.

'Tomorrow we go back to Lhasa,' I tell him, 'and we will have to separate. We have experienced something beautiful together, but let's not try to prolong it. You are married and you have a child. You will go back to Beijing, back to your life, and I will return to mine. Let's leave the memory of our encounter here, in Tibet. If we see each other again, we will destroy it.'

He presses my hand gently.

'I am happy to have met you.'

'I am happy to have known you.'

He holds me in his arms. It's a brave gesture, since just fifty metres away our chaperones are watching us. In another society we could be together.

How enchanted I am by this first love in my life as a woman, how different it is from the rushed fumbles I have known with men. A man seduces a woman differently, he courts her and takes his time – even though the woman isn't fooled and knows that she will end up in bed with him.

I will meet Mr X again – he will help me set up my dance company – but, romantically, nothing more will happen between us.

To distract me during my long convalescence, a friend from the Guangdong Dance Academy invites me to collaborate with her husband who has opened a nightclub in Beijing. My job is to organize rock concerts and dance shows so I bring in the famous Chinese band *Lingdian* (Zero Point), and I also get some of the alumni from the Academy's modern dance class to present shows at the club – they can't get work in Beijing, since most dance companies only stage traditional work. With them I decide to establish a modern dance troupe, the Beijing Modern Dance Company, under the auspices of the Beijing Cultural Bureau.

The rehearsals for our first show, *Black and Red*, are particularly exhausting for me as I have decided to take on a dancing role, my first since the operation. I have to adapt the choreography to my diminished capabilities. I am still limping and my legs are different temperatures: the right one is normal, but the left leg is cold and numb, because the blood doesn't circulate properly.

'Miss AC/DC plays *Black and Red*'. Two weeks before the dress rehearsal this headline explodes onto the front page of the *China Youth Daily* and makes me suffocate with rage. The national television channel CCTV, which broadcasts in English, happens to be sending a crew to film me and this gives me the perfect opportunity to take my revenge. I drag the camera crew to the offices of the *China Youth Daily* and demand to see the editor in chief.

'"Miss AC/DC!" How dare you? It's an insult! If you don't withdraw that headline, I'll sue you for libel.'

The editor in chief tries to justify himself, but is visibly shaken in front of the cameras. The segment about me is broadcast during that evening's news and the next day the *China Youth Daily* publishes an apology. But the journalist goes on the offensive again and this time he writes to the head of the Beijing Cultural Bureau to complain about a transsexual having the audacity to show herself on a Beijing stage. The director defends himself, sends a delegation to the rehearsals to observe our work, and concludes that 'Jin Xing is a serious dancer and her company does quality work'.

But the battle is not yet won. In spite of the director's thumbs up, rumours abound that our show is anti-communist. In the offices of the Cultural Bureau, the clerk points to the headline in the *China Youth Daily*.

'*Black and Red* is a confusing title, don't you think?' He looks up at me with unfocused eyes. 'For instance... Hmmm... Couldn't it be an expression of antagonism between the Party and an opponent? Red, the Party; Black, the enemy of the people?'

Those civil servants are so literal I could cry.

'Not at all.'

'Isn't it also the title of the French writer Stendhal's famous novel? Could it be by any chance an adaptation of that work?'

'Neither. It's a modern dance ballet. The dancers are dressed in black and hold red fans in their hands. The title describes the colours used on stage. It's as simple as that.'

He looks sceptical. I go on.

'It's an artistic creation which, I can assure you, doesn't have a hint of politics about it.'

He nods his head, but I can tell he's still not convinced.

It's time to pull some powerful strings and I call on Mr X, the man from Lhasa. He has not forgotten me and actually sounds happy to hear from me. I explain that I am producing a modern dance show, the first one in the People's Republic, and that it has come up against some political problems. I ask for his protection, and wonder if he has friends in the Propaganda Department he could call on. The warmth in his voice reminds me of our illicit liaison at the hot springs. Yes, he does have a very good friend at the Propaganda Department and he will ask him to send a representative to the rehearsals.

'Don't worry. Everything will be fine. Good luck with your project.'

And so a new group of civil servants sits down solemnly on the benches in the studio to pronounce upon the political acceptability of our show. Once again, we receive a green light.

Finally, it is the dress rehearsal. Normally this would be closed to the general public, with only the critics in attendance, but on this occasion more than a hundred reporters and about twenty photographers have gathered at the foot of the stage. When the curtain rises, the shutter clicks from the cameras drown out the music and the flashbulbs blind us. Tickets for the premiere on the following night sell on the black market for triple the original price. Talk about no such thing as bad publicity! The theatre crackles with energy, which we can feel ripple all the way backstage, and it pushes me to challenge myself, to forget the pain that still throbs through me whenever I put my left foot down. Within thirty seconds, my whole leg begins to shake. At the end of each number, a chiropractor waits for me in the wings ready to massage me to stimulate the blood circulation. Only my closest friends know that I am still in pain and I want it to stay that way; the audience must not notice my weakness. When we take our bows at the end of the show, the audience jumps to its feet and applauds loudly. They didn't suspect a thing! The curtain calls last for twenty minutes... It is a mind-blowing and proud moment for me.

Children surround me on the set of a TV show devoted to *Black and Red*. Their parents recognize me and ask for my autograph. A little boy approaches and touches my sleeve.

'Madame Xing, Madame Xing, my mum said you were a man before. Is it true?'

'It's true.'

'And now you are a woman.'

'Madame Xing wasn't happy when she was a man. Now she is happy to be a woman.'

The little boy stares at me, his mouth wide open.

'Can we change too?'

'No! You are perfect the way you are. You don't need to change.'

This and other projects make me forget my bad leg. I choreograph a new show for Cheng Fangyuan – *The Sound of Music*, the first musical to be staged in China – and I enjoy it enormously. The dance company takes up all my energy. I run it like an army school, with an emphasis on discipline, rigour and intense work. Even though it is modern dance, I do not want to lose the virtuosity and precision that are the hallmarks of traditional Chinese dance. I must guide the dancers with a firm hand in order to make them gel and become a harmonious company.

Fan, one of the company dancers, serves as my assistant and stays in my house while he is looking for his own apartment. I meet D through him – they did their military service together in Lanzhou. Physically, D is my ideal man: tall (1.87 metres), athletic (he plays in one of China's best handball teams), and with a chiselled face and sensual lips; he is much more handsome even than the actor Chow Yun-Fat. We fall in love and he moves into my place as well. But no sooner has he moved in than Fan falls into a temper, with raging fits; he throws things at the walls. He tries to turn D against me and D can't understand why I let him stay. Too late, I realize that Fan's angry outbursts are ill-disguised fits of jealousy. He is gay and has been in love with D since their time together in military service. By now the cracks are beginning to show in my relationship with D.

Physical beauty doesn't necessarily go hand in hand with intellectual finesse and, like most Chinese men, D lives in the past. After three months, he packs up and leaves.

Fan, however, is still raging against me. At rehearsals, he sulks and sabotages the work. At the end of a particularly poor session, I gather the company together for a meeting.

'If you are as apathetic tomorrow as you are today, you can all look for another job.'

The following Saturday, at two or three in the morning, I am woken by urgent knocks on my door. Fan, blind-drunk, almost falls into my arms.

'What do you want?'

'Speak with you.'

'You're stewed to the gills. Go away. We'll speak tomorrow.'

But his foot is wedged in the door and I can't close it so I let him in. He pulls a hammer from his pocket and begins to smash everything within reach: chairs, tables, paintings, mirrors. He applies himself to his mission of destruction with the rigid determination of an automaton and all I can do is watch him without a word. No use trying to interfere, the hammer would end up between my eyes. When he slows down, I lift my arm to stop him and he grabs me by the neck.

'Why did you lie to me?'

'What are you talking about?'

'Why aren't you taking me to Taiwan?'

'The trip has been cancelled, you know that.'

'So why do you keep talking about it to the dancers?'

'It's to motivate them, to push them to work harder.'

'You lie to us. You manipulate us.'

I shrug.

His rage picks up again. He hits me with the back of his hand

and, staggering, grabs my nightgown and rips it apart as he falls. I pull away and go to my bedroom to change. When I come back into the living room he is on his knees, sobbing. Then he suddenly flips over and falls asleep on the carpet. I have never seen such a drunkard. Such lack of character and dignity! I pick up the shards of glass, pieces of wood and other detritus of my destroyed furniture and artefacts, then sit down on the balcony to read and keep an eye on him. After a while he wakes up and leaves, without even looking at me.

On Monday, Fan barges into the studio with three other dancers.

'No warm-up this morning. We need to talk to you.'

'Excuse me? So now you're making the decisions?'

'We want some changes.'

'What kind of changes?'

'Firstly, you are way too demanding. You yell at us all the time, and you don't let the girls rest when they have their periods. Secondly, you are both the company director and the artistic director. Thirdly, you are too autocratic; you don't let us create our own dances.'

I burst out laughing.

'So those are your demands? Fine. Number one: OK, I yell at you, but it's during rehearsal, for professional reasons, to get the best performances from you. Do you know of a single choreographer who doesn't lose her temper with her dancers? As for the girls' periods, believe me, abroad, girls dance every day, period or no period, no excuse! Number two: I am the company director. Your contract specifies that you must receive a monthly salary, plus a bonus for each performance. Have I ever missed a payment? Have I ever been late giving you a bonus? I have not and never will be. However, there is nothing in the contract that requires me to divulge the company's income. Number three: I am the artistic director. If you wish to choreograph your own dances, there is nothing to stop you from doing so in your own free time.'

I am rather satisfied with my little speech. Their demands make no sense: it is obvious that Fan has simply turned them against me.

'What do you really want?'

'No more hierarchy,' says one of the girls.

'To get rid of you,' spits Fan, his face twisted with hate.

I stand up.

'And you think it's enough to say "Stop!" for the whole earth to quit turning? You're fired, the four of you. I will submit my decision to the Cultural Bureau.'

By chance, the Cultural Bureau is in plenary session when I arrive, and they listen to me in dead silence, with only the occasional clearing of the throat and sideways look, as if Fan had turned them against me too! Faced with such lack of support I hand in my resignation.

A month later, the director of the Cultural Bureau calls me up. They need me to take care of the salaries.

'The salaries? But I resigned a month ago! I am not part of the company any more. You'll have to manage without me.'

'Jin Xing, you forget you are in a communist country. You depend on the Party and the Ministry of Culture. You are not abroad any more, you cannot do whatever you feel like.'

'So you need me? You don't trust me, but as soon as you have a problem, you whistle and expect me to come running? Go to hell – you, the Ministry and the Party – and leave me alone.'

The news spreads like wildfire. Fan, who still has access to my address book, lets the entire press know that I am out; journalists call up the Cultural Bureau and the dancers to get final confirmation. Nobody, including me, offers any explanation. It is the only way to let the story die away. But what bitter disappointment, to have run a company for three years, to have produced successful shows like *Black and Red*, only to end up with this fiasco!

The company does not survive my departure. I learn later that the director of the Beijing Cultural Bureau yelled at the dancers, 'You are idiots. You brought down Jin Xing, but she was the one who had top billing, she was the name the audience wanted to see. Without her, your company is nothing.'

⌒

One night as I am having dinner with friends at The Hacienda, a Spanish restaurant, one of them says, 'Jin Xing, you know everybody in Beijing, you speak English… you should open a bar.'

'And who would finance it?'

'Me,' replies Zheng Hao, another friend, who works at MTV. 'I'll lend you the money.'

Within a week I find a space of around 400 square metres in the embassy quarter and I design it like the set for a ballet or an opera, using a mixture of stone and wood, and decorating it with Chinese sculptures and a statue of an Indonesian goddess whose womanly body tapers into a snake's tail. I call the bar Half-Dream, like my ballet. My singer friends perform on the stage and we play jazz, blues and Latin–American music. On the opening night there are so many diplomats' cars outside the entrance that they block the street.

I spend my evenings at Half-Dream surrounded by friends, exactly as I would do in my own living room. You can always find me at table thirteen – my lucky number – which can be screened off with curtains. Sometimes I'm there in the afternoons too, reading a book. My friends stop by, ask, 'Is Jin Xing there?', and sit down with me for a drink.

One day my assistant tells me she has found a special tea that we should serve at the bar. I am intrigued.

'They sell it at the herbal store. It's erectile tea – they say it gives you a hard-on.'

We double up with laughter.

'Well, run and buy some, quick.'

From then on, the waiters ask the customers in a discreet voice, 'Sir, would you like some erectile tea?'

I have no idea if the tea is effective or not, but it's one of our most popular drinks and becomes part of our reputation.

There is a rush of diplomats and Westerners and some Chinese come too, those we call the 'nouveaux riches' though they have kept their less refined ways. They ask for hostesses to keep them company, but I don't have hostesses working for me. In fact, in order to avoid any misunderstandings, I only hire waiters.

'But doesn't Jin Xing work here?'

'Yes, but don't look for Jin Xing the dancer. Here I am the boss – and the only woman.'

A group of pot-bellied men sit with a freshly brewed pot of our special tea.

'You're going to go bankrupt, you know. Bring us some playing cards, at least. We're going to play poker.'

'Sorry, but this is not a gambling den. Cards are forbidden here.'

They are so loud, the Chinese, when they play poker in bars. Such a racket! You can't hear the music, you can't even hear yourself speak. It ruins the atmosphere entirely.

'Come on, Jin Xing, bend the rules a little! Don't you want to make money?'

'I don't care. I don't do any shady business.'

'Come on, get us a pack of cards, will you?'

'Give me three hundred thousand *yuan* and I'll get them printed for you.'

I hone my image as a femme fatale who won't let herself be pushed around. They say I am self-assured like a man, but there are women who also have this kind of confidence. I pick the feminine characteristics that work for me and I keep my masculine qualities. In a picture of me taken at the bar, I am sitting, pensive, dressed in a long garnet-coloured skirt discreetly revealing my ankles, with a fur cape caressing my shoulders. It is a romantic pose, of course, but it also shows that I am also unmistakably the boss.

That balance is not always easy to achieve. I feel like a wild teenager testing out her power over men. It's exciting. I have several lovers at the same time: German, French, English and Arab. I flirt like a man. Straightforward. I know right away what they want: I know men! I respond tit for tat, but I never make the first move.

There is no need for me to say anything – they would never realize – but I prefer to put my cards on the table right away, before things go too far.

'I have to tell you something. I am different from other women.'

'Yes, absolutely you're quite different.'

'No, I mean, I am really different.'

'What do you mean?'

'I was a man, before.'

'No!'

'Yes, it's true.'

Some men are turned on by it. Others turn away. What can I do? I can't change my past.

Half-Dream is the most fashionable bar in Beijing. Rock bands like Cui Jian and Lingdian give concerts on the stage, and I organize special events like Hungarian Week, featuring Hungarian rock and cuisine, and an International Festival of Short Films. And I act in my first film there.

In 1997 I played a Mongolian princess on the stage, in a drama based on a true story from the Genghis Khan era, about a young woman who cuts off her hand and buries it with the body of her husband who was killed by the enemy. A year later, a filmmaker asks me to play myself in a semi-fictional documentary he is directing about the arts in Beijing. The film is called *The Angel and the Fever*. It features a Japanese man who comes to Beijing looking for a young Chinese soldier he had known when he was a little boy. The Japanese man meets a painter, then a TV director from CCTV, and then a rock singer who takes him to Half-Dream. 'The owner of Half-Dream knows everybody,' he tells him. 'She'll be able to help you.' The Japanese man gets a job as a dishwasher and one night he shows me the photo of the little Chinese soldier. 'Could you help me find him? I knew him twenty years ago.' The photo is a picture of me when I was at the army school. I tell the Japanese man, 'This little boy is me.'

Zheng Hao has invested a lot of money in the bar so he hires his sister to do the accounts. Our ideas are very different. My concept for Half-Dream is that it should offer luxury services for top-end customers, just like a five-star hotel: imported red wine, impeccably laundered napkins and the best liquor. Zheng Hao's sister, however, puts the brakes on my expenditure. After a year, I give up the fight to impose my vision on the bar. Anyway, the role of Night Queen is becoming a strain. I miss dancing and the stage.

⌒

March 2000. I land at Shanghai airport with half my dance company and four suitcases. We don't have anywhere to stay, only the address of a cheap hotel, but the balmy air and the excitement of a new adventure thrill me.

The Shanghai adventure started with an offer from Chen Bangke, a financier associated with the Propaganda Department who also sponsors the Shanghai Opera. First, he asked me to choreograph the famous revolutionary ballet *Sister Jiang*; but I had decided long ago not to do any more propaganda shows, and anyway I already had a commitment to develop a ballet with the Shaolin monks, *The Powerful Winds of Shaolin*, to present in Bangkok at the millennium celebrations at the request of the Thai royal family. I had a better idea, however, and I put it to him. The previous year I had produced *The Peony Pavilion*, the famous Kunju Opera composed at the end of the Ming Dynasty. It tells the story of an official's daughter and her love for a poor young scholar. What if we adapted *The Peony Pavilion* into a modern dance ballet?

Chen Bangke likes the idea, but when we start rehearsing it is a disaster: the dancers from the Shanghai Opera are trained only in traditional dance. For three months I try to teach them the basics of modern dance, but they are not ready. In June, I fly the remaining members of my company to Shanghai and produce another show: *Shanghai Tango*. I have based the choreography for this dance on a famous Chinese play that reveals the emotional struggles of a woman in one of China's very ancient families. It speaks to me of the same struggles that the women of Shanghai face today; it resonates with my own struggles, too. I use the narrative to make a connection between Chinese women through the centuries – and it works. It is popular beyond my wildest dreams.

My friends had predicted I wouldn't last more than three days in the cultural desert of Shanghai. A huge economic and financial centre, Shanghai is growing at a lightning pace, but censorship suffocates the arts and creatively it's ten years behind Beijing. However, I love it there. My apartment is tiny, the heat is stifling, but the city is welcoming and the challenge of breathing new life into the Opera House, whose reputation has declined over the last twenty years, increases my energy tenfold.

Shanghai Tango is such a success that the director of the Opera House becomes afraid that I will want to take his place at the helm. I quit – I have had enough of fighting and trying to persuade people that their fears are unfounded – and I set up the Jin Xing Dance Theatre with Chen Bangke's support.

⸺

My birthday is 13 August and three days after I turn thirty-four (thirty-three according to the Western calendar), my mother calls me. Her voice sounds different, calmer.

'There's something you're not telling me.'

Silence. Suddenly I have a premonition.

'Oh my God. You've found a child for me.'

'Yes, Jin Xing. You are a mum.'

We had talked about it a long time ago and this had been her plan all along. What if I said no, would she keep the baby?

'You're not saying anything?'

What to say? I am speechless.

'Is it a boy or a girl? Is it in good health?'

The astrologer's prediction comes back to me. I would have a child the year I turned thirty-three, she had said.

'A boy,' my mother says. 'In good health.'

'He is with you?'

'Yes.'

I can't describe it; I am overjoyed.

He is asleep in my arms and I am sitting down, for fear of dropping him. His black hair is glued down with sweat and he gives off the musky smell of a young creature. His closed eyes are two tiny slits above the plump folds of his cheeks. His tiny fingers wrap around my index finger and a smile floats on his lips. I look at my mother who is observing us together. Tears run down my cheeks, but I don't dare wipe them off in case I wake him. I am petrified.

'Tell me.'

His mother is a soldier in the People's Liberation Army. She is twenty-one. His father is a married officer. She was hoping that the arrival of the baby would push him to divorce, but he changed his mind. In China it is usually the baby girls that are abandoned: you can find them everywhere, even in ditches in the countryside. But it's rare to abandon a boy. Everyone wanted him. My mother had been to visit a sick friend at the Beijing Naval Hospital the day he was born and the mother placed her little boy in my mother's arms. Two dimples appeared in his chubby cheeks – a good omen.

'Auntie, do you want him?' asked the mother.

'Would you give him to me?'

'Auntie, you are too old. How could you raise him?'

My mother is sixty-three. She explains that he would not live with her, but with her daughter, who can't have children.

Leo, or Dudu – his Chinese name is Jin Zi Yong – was born on 29 July. He has been at my mother's home for two weeks. She was afraid to let me know, in case I didn't want him.

She lets me change him. You have to hold the baby firmly with one hand while folding the dirty nappy with the other. Then, gathering the tiny ankles between the fingers of the first hand, you slip the clean nappy under the baby's buttocks with a quick, gentle movement. I concentrate hard. Leo lets me change him without crying. His eyes don't leave me, as though he is wondering if he can trust me. Will I stick the pin into his ribs? I don't. I wrap the swaddling cloth over the nappy and pin it tight, but not too tight. He hasn't cried once.

My mother looks at me with astonishment.

'Where did you learn how to do that?'

I hold him against my chest. His head is resting in the crook of my arm. He gurgles, perhaps satisfied that I have accomplished my task so flawlessly. His mouth, half-open, presses against my breast. I smile at him and slip a finger between his lips.

'It came by itself.'

Before Leo I was like a pretty, colourful kite that floated freely in the wind. Now Leo holds the kite strings with a firm hand. I come home to him every night and I don't party as I used to in Beijing. On an Internet site dedicated to me, people have differing opinions. Some say, 'Oh, Jin Xing, what a big heart!' Others snipe, 'You must be kidding. It's all for show. She's monstrously selfish. The baby will be extremely disturbed.' I say nothing. Let them think what they want.

In October, I produce Carl Orff's *Carmina Burana* with my dance company. The text is based on a collection of poems and songs written in Latin by Benedictine monks in the thirteenth century. They are poems of desire. Rather than following the Latin text, I let the music be my guide. In my version, love is forbidden by the group. A man and a woman fall in love, and while the man caves in to the group's pressure, the woman continues to sing of her love until the group punishes her for it. My story is about the conflict between group values and individuality. The sensuality is expressed in a very oriental way. To evoke nudity, a gauze hides the girls from the audience, concealing all but their legs and their feet. Later they sit at a table fitted with wheels while the men, standing at a distance, wave long bamboo canes in their direction. There is never any contact between them, only this male gesture of desire.

Black and Red, Shanghai Tango and *Carmina Burana* are international productions, and we take them on tour both within Asia – to Korea, Hong Kong and Macau – and beyond, to Germany, France and Belgium. When I tour in Europe I always wonder if my style will be appreciated, if perhaps the critics might find it passé – after all, China is not at the forefront of modern dance – but I dance for the public, not for the critics. In my opinion, the modern dance world has become too intellectual. It is discouraging for the spectators.

At the end of 2001, the French TV channel Arté broadcast a documentary about me directed by a French filmmaker. So now, when I tour in France, many spectators know who I am. 'Oh, it's the People's Army colonel, the transsexual!' In Marseilles, in Lille, in Paris, people are curious. They come and talk to me after the show. 'So that's Chinese modern dance?'

There are four of us in the family now. After Leo comes Mimi. She was born in Manchuria, in Shenyang, my hometown, also the product of a love affair that turned sour. The lovers were both married to other people and had talked of divorcing and marrying each other if the baby was a boy. When it turned out to be a girl, they didn't want her. My mother knew I wanted another child and, thank God, the single-child policy doesn't apply to adoptions.

'It's a girl, do you want her?'

I was in Germany this time, on tour, and I said yes right away. As long as she was healthy. Her Chinese name is Jin Zi Han. I don't think her mother had a good pregnancy because whenever I gave her a bottle her little hands would hold onto it in a vice-like grip, and she would cry if I ever left her alone.

A year later, two friends of my mother's were talking about an eighteen-year-old student from Beijing University who was five months pregnant. The father was also a student in Beijing. They could not keep the baby, and so Julian joined us. We call him Xiao Sir, Little Sir, because he is the youngest. His Chinese name is Jin Zi Xung. He is a solid little guy.

Three children is a big responsibility. A single mother cannot quit her job and it is a constant struggle to keep the dance company afloat. I could not have raised my children and worked full-time if I had continued my night owl existence in Beijing. I only go to the most important gala banquets and dinners now – all my energy is devoted to the children and my work.

In 2002 I buy a house in the former French Concession neighbourhood in the heart of Shanghai. It is deep inside a compound of three-storey houses where foreign bankers used to live in the thirties. When the communists came into power in 1949 the houses were requisitioned as lodgings for employees of the Ministry of Culture and Propaganda. The house I buy once belonged to a family who were moving to the United States. It has a little garden.

I have a pistachio-green Volkswagen Beetle which I drive to my studio at the Opera House each morning. I have ordered a Porsche Cayenne for the family: with two servants, we are six, so we need a big car. One day I will put the Beetle into storage and then give it to Mimi as a present when she turns eighteen. I dream of a mauve-coloured Maserati. I would buy it purely for my own pleasure, like a ring with a precious stone to decorate the hand.

October 2002, Paris. I push open the door of Le Bon Marché, the elegant department store where I have come to do some shopping with a Chinese friend. Just back from Berlin, I am dressed in my movie-star get-up: long coat almost to the ground, little bag, gloves.

'Oh, *pardon!*'

The tall, dark, Mediterranean-looking man who stepped into the revolving doors ahead of us pulls back to let us go first.

'Ladies, please, after you.'

He smiles at us. We nod to him and sweep into the art nouveau store. We sail between the Louis Vuitton bags and Annick Goutal perfumes, then walk up to the third floor to explore the couture collections. Halfway up, in the lingerie department, my friend whispers in my ear, 'Don't turn around, it's the man we saw earlier. He's following us.' She elbows me to signal that he is already behind us.

'Excuse me, aren't you the Chinese dancer?'

I turn towards him, pretending not to know what he is talking about.

'No.'

We are shopping. I am not in the mood to be cornered by a clingy man.

His face turns red and he bows politely, although his eyes remain fixed on me.

'I'm so sorry. I thought... Please forgive me. You looked like someone else... I was wrong. May I invite you for a drink?'

He is cute with his brown hair and his dark eyes, and elegant too, with a bit of an Italian look, which I like, but I don't want to drop my friend.

'No thank you; it's very nice of you, but we are travelling. We don't have the time.'

He introduces himself as Guillaume.

'Would you at least give me your phone number? Perhaps I can call you later?'

'Oh! It's a Chinese mobile. There are too many digits!'

He insists so politely, though, that I give in.

'OK, if you like. I'll take your card. I will try to call you later.'

A few days before returning to Shanghai, my friend throws a party and I give him a call. He is so sorry, he cannot make it. He is on duty that night: he does security at the Enghien-les-Bains casino. What bad luck.

From Hainan Island in the south of China, where I spend my end-of-year vacation with Dudu, I call my European friends to wish them Merry Christmas. I see Guillaume's name in my book and I dial it. It will surprise him.

'Merry Christmas from China!'

He is stunned. I can tell from his voice that he never thought he would hear from me again. And also that he is thrilled he was wrong. We decide to meet in Paris.

'So you *were* the Chinese dancer from the film,' he says. 'The documentary they showed on Arté. Don't lie to me.'

He looks at me sideways and raises his eyebrows. He has a mocking smile. I make a mock-sorry face.

His family is originally from Italy and transsexuals fascinate him. He tells me about this bar in Paris, the T-Club, where the transsexuals are more beautiful, more feminine even than 'real' women. But they are half-operated and they look like transvestites, with too much make-up: vulgar. They are fine to spend a night with, but he would never date one.

'But you. You are different.'

He stares at me. It seems that ever since seeing the documentary he has dreamt of meeting me. He is convinced that I am his ideal woman. For me he is the ideal lover, but I am not sure he is the ideal man. He is a playboy, a man who won't stay still. We see each other again in Paris, each time I tour in Europe, and he visits me in Shanghai. The children love him. But back in France, he resumes his wanderings. With my three children, I need a serious man, someone I can count on. A father.

⁓

The man at Charles de Gaulle airport with the orange tie, the tall blond man talking to the Air France employee who has just sat on the bench not far from me – is not French; I would bet on it. He looks too serious. A Frenchman cannot see a woman without flirting with her. He looks northern European. English? German? I can't think about him any more because they have announced boarding. I grab Uttika, my chihuahua, who is yapping in her bag – the Louis Vuitton dog bag I have just bought to match my cosmetics bag – and get a quick glimpse of him as I pass by. I have just had my hair cut, which is why I am running late. The stylist came over at 7.30 p.m., the appointed time. In China, when you have long hair and you decide to cut it, you must choose a propitious date and time. At 9.30 p.m. the cut was finished, but the taxi driver had to step on the gas to get me to the airport in time for the midnight flight. I think the fringe is particularly becoming. It comes down in a point between my eyebrows, which makes my face look like a heart framed by chin-length hair.

I take my seat in first class with Uttika and the man with the orange tie reappears and sits down next to me. What a surprise! Usually in first class you get ugly old men. He still doesn't say anything, so I initiate conversation.

'My chihuahua is not in your way, I hope?'

'No, no, not at all. Please. What a sweet little dog! What's his name?'

The flight lasts twelve hours so we have plenty of time to get to know each other. He lives in Shanghai and works for Saint-Gobain, the French glass-manufacturing company. He is German and his name is Hans-Gert. On Air France first-class passengers get creamy cotton pyjamas designed by Christian Lacroix to wear for the night. We change in the bathrooms and lie down on our bed-style seats, both in identical pyjamas, like an old couple. We laugh about it. The next morning, we wake up at the same time and look at each other. His hand on mine is warm. The flight attendants pass by with the breakfast trolley and the smell of French coffee wafts through the plane.

'I would like this flight to never end,' I tell him.

He smiles at me.

His Chinese girlfriend is picking him up at the airport. I try to sober up. There are moments that are not meant to last. But he calls me the next day. He has broken up with his girlfriend. Can he come and see me?

I wait for him at the entrance to the compound to show him where to park, Julian in my arms. I invite him into my small living room. He sits down on the four-poster bed that serves as a couch. Julian sits at his feet and stares at him, then climbs up on his lap and runs his little fingers along his cheek. Hans-Gert smiles and lets him do it. We sit down at the table for a dinner of Shanghai specialities.

'I am not a simple woman, you know. My story is a little complicated.'

He puts down his chopsticks to listen to me. His face expresses only fascination, even more interest than before. As I tell him, I see his eyes veil over. Who could be prepared for such a revelation? We end the meal. He stays a little longer, then politely says goodbye. From the door I watch him deftly reverse his car up the narrow alley. Will he be one of those men who find my story so perturbing that he won't come back?

He calls me again the next day.

'I want to see you again.'

He takes care of the children like an adoring dad. From the big window in the Thai restaurant where we have just had lunch, I watch him play with them on the garden lawn. He is tender and attentive, as he is with me. This is the family I have dreamt of.

And yet Guillaume still calls me every day and I cannot forget him. Why this wish for family life? I can take care of the children by myself, with the servants' help. I don't need a man. Many women raise their children by themselves. In any case I will never have a traditional family. If I stay single, I can have all the lovers I want. Am I so worried that people will say 'she is a transsexual, she cannot get married, no man will want her'? Is it so important for me to convince the Chinese that I have a real family and that I am a woman just like the others? Do I want to get married for the children or to keep the gossips quiet?

A Thai seer, famous for the accuracy of his predictions, has come to Shanghai to study the feng shui of a building being constructed by a major investment company. During the dinner, to which I am invited, he tells me, 'I watched you when you locked your car. You looked around you first to make sure the coast was clear. You must have been in the army. You keep people at a certain distance and you know how to control situations. Even if a situation turns out badly, you know how to hold on to your position. You have the power to create your own fate. You will found an empire – in jewels, perfumes, real estate, or similar. You will marry four times. And you will end up with an Asian man, who will be very good to you.'

Throughout my life, whenever I have wished very hard for something, my dream has come true. When I was in the army, my fate was all planned out. If I had stayed on those tracks, I would have simply become a star dancer in the PLA troupe. We all have the choice to get off one train and jump onto another one heading for a more beautiful destination. By becoming a woman I have changed tracks. I had to do it. It was a difficult and treacherous journey, but that was the only way I could realize my childhood dream. And the arrival of the children has taken me to another platform.

I feel like the heir of one of those heroines of Chinese history, those women who were born into poverty and branded immoral by society, but challenged the fate to which they were condemned. Women like Xai Jin Hua, a peasant girl from Zughou who lived alone with her mother near a magnificent, touristy lake towards the end of the nineteenth century, during the Qing Dynasty. At the age of sixteen she is beautiful but very poor, so she and a friend get the idea to entertain the tourists like Japanese geisha, by serenading them from a boat and serving them drinks. Governor Hong, a married, middle-aged, high-ranking government official, falls in love with Xai Jin Hua and takes her as his mistress. When the emperor sends the governor to Berlin to be his ambassador, the governor's wife refuses to exile herself among those blonde people with long noses, so Governor Hong takes his mistress instead. In Berlin, Xai Jin Hua learns German, English and French and charms the king's entire court. Three years later, their mission accomplished, they travel back to China. Unfortunately, Governor Hong dies suddenly upon his return to Beijing, and the legitimate spouse throws out her rival. With a mournful heart Xai Jin Hua returns to Zughou, but her childhood friend has a new idea: why don't they open a brothel in Shanghai? So Xai Jin Hua becomes the most famous madam in town. All the intellectuals and politicians come and visit her. However, the governor's wife is still jealous and arranges to have the brothel destroyed by a gangster. Banned from Shanghai, Xai Jin Hua opens another brothel in Tianjin, a harbour town near Beijing, just at the time when the war with the foreign allies starts, following the Boxer Rebellion. Thanks to her knowledge of German, Xai Jin Hua is able to save the empress's life and helps to negotiate peace between the Germans and the Chinese, but the Chinese government feels humiliated to have been saved by a prostitute and instead of thanking her, they throw her into jail.

She is eventually released and lives to a grand old age in Beijing.

My other heroine is Madame Mao, the wife of Chairman Mao. She was a Shanghai actress in the forties – not a very talented one, and not even really beautiful, but nevertheless she was full of charm and intelligence. Realizing that her career was not taking off, she decided to join the communists in the countryside. What a godsend for Mao: a young Shanghai actress leaves the Kuomintang to join the Revolution! She became his mistress, then his wife. But Mao was a ladies' man and soon turned his attention to other women. Furious at being neglected, she threw all her energy into the arts and produced the ten major masterpieces of the Cultural Revolution.

I would like to emulate one of those heroines. I would like to be the type of woman who carves out her own destiny and becomes a princess. I think we all choreograph our lives, in the end – improvising, adapting, trying out new characters and forms, striving to give the best performance we can, until the final curtain falls.